Crumbs
FOR
LIFE

Inspirational Devotions

BY

LaCountess B. Corbitt

DEDICATION

I n honor of God's Holy presence in my life I dedicate this devotional to His greatness and omnipotence, Willie A. Corbitt and Ernestine Corbitt (mother deceased) my parents that God entrusted my life and rearing to and to my children that I wholeheartedly love, adore and appreciate the opportunity to parent Gary E. Pridgeon, Jr., Darea S. Pridgeon, Michael T. Pridgeon,, Pastor John K. Jenkins, Sr. for all the spiritual guidance, leadership and discipleship training.

FORWARD

Dear Bonnie,

I t is with immense joy and pride that I find myself tasked
with the honor of penning a few words for your upcom-
ing book. As I sit down to write this forward, I am overwhelmed by a sense of anticipation and excitement, knowing
that readers are about to embark on a journey of discovery,
insight, and perhaps, a touch of the extraordinary.

From the earliest conversations about your book to witnessing
the countless hours of dedication and passion you poured into
its creation, I have had a front-row seat to the evolution of
your literary endeavor. Your words, like a carefully woven tap-
estry, have the power to transport readers to realms unknown,
challenge their perspectives, and, most importantly, resonate
with the core of their being.

In the pages that follow, readers will undoubtedly encounter
the essence of your unique voice — a voice that speaks not

only from the depths of your experiences but also from the wellspring of your imagination. It is a voice that carries the weight of authenticity, the nuance of empathy, and the resonance of universal truths.

Bonnie, what strikes me most about your literary prowess is the courage embedded in your words. Your willingness to explore the complexities of the human condition, to dive into the shadows and illuminate the light within, is a testament to your artistic integrity. In a world that sometimes shies away from uncomfortable truths, your book stands as a beacon of authenticity and vulnerability.

This book is not merely a collection of words on paper but a manifestation of your creative spirit and the culmination of your artistic evolution. It is an offering to the world, an invitation for readers to connect, reflect, and, perhaps, be transformed.

May this book find its way into the hearts and minds of readers, leaving an indelible mark on their souls. Here's to the boundless potential of your storytelling, the impact of your narrative, and the adventures that await those who turn the pages of your creation.

Congratulations, my friend, on this literary milestone. May your book soar to heights as infinite as the stories it holds.

Warmest Regards,

Pastor Duane E. Dickens Sr. aka Pastor D

Bonnie Corbitt inspires many people who have been following her blog. Her writing encourages her readers to know how to get through life with a positive attitude and faith. She loves sharing with others about the Lord. She is a dedicated daughter who lovingly cares for her father. She is also a loving mother and friend to many.

Rev. Lettie Carr, Esq., Director

Ministry and Administrative Support Services

& Contract Administrator

First Baptist Church of Glenarden

❧ Greetings Ms. Corbitt!!

I love you so very much, and I truly thank God for allowing us to meet as co-workers at First Baptist Church of Glenarden.

I not only thank you for always "teaching me how to use my computer effectively" but you empowered me by sharing your knowledge of scriptures as well.

Ms. Bonnie, what I admired most about you were your daily scripture writings and teachings about God's word. I was truly elevated by your knowledge and the manner in which you carried out His word.

Then COVID came upon the earth. I remember that you and I were at the staff retreat in February, planning how we were going to protect our families IF the spread of COVID continued. It continued and the church closed in March. It was through our pre-planning that we had built up an arsenal of gloves, masks, sanitizers, etc. (I still have a supply of these elements ready today - just in case).

Bonnie, I could go on and on about our wonderful relationship in Christ, however, we will continue asking God to bless our families and living for Him daily.

"ENJOY THE MOMENT!"

Helen Cheston Bryant

ABOUT THE AUTHOR

L aCountess B Corbitt (Bonnie) has over forty years of Christian experience at a rapidly growing mega Church. She has attended and participated in discipleship classes and ministries and personal life experiences of which she has acquired wisdom, knowledge and understanding of the Word of God. After years of sharing daily life circumstances alongside scripture and moral principles, many encouraged her to compile these thoughts in a book.

It has always been her desire to inspire, uplift and encourage others. She is a faithful believer who trusts in God's Word and Promises.

TABLE OF CONTENTS

PREFACE

C rumbs for Life is devoted to life circumstances, personal issues, relationships, and moral values based on
scripture. The devotions are random and cannot be specifically
categorized, but will touch base with all life challenges. My desire and focus are to target all ages, anyone who can read with
understanding and desire to accomplish a greater understanding and deeper personal relations with God, as well as recognition of unrighteous character traits. Readers will either find
a devotion to apply to their life presently or find one that will
relate to a challenging past or a nougat for future reference.

ACKNOWLEDGMENTS

D aily, I share inspirational readings with others. Although I am not a licensed minister, I enjoy reading scripture and religious documentary. I desire to share wisdom and knowledge acquired during my spiritual growth in Christ and personal experiences. If, in any way, I can inspire or give someone a new perspective in viewing or dealing with the trials and storms that approach them daily, it is a blessing. I have found reading Daily Devotionals to be inspiring and, enlightening and the reading of uplifting to my spirit. When you need encouragement, God has a word for every situation.

When I read devotions, I must admit that often they apply to a present need. I trust and know that God directed the selection to cross my path to inspire me or enlighten me to share and inspire someone else. I can give someone hope in a situation where they may have any doubt. God will be pleased with me and will be pleased knowing that I have assisted in some way. As we grow in our walk with God, it is a good practice to incorporate spiritual readings and guidance daily in addition to our personal devotional time with God and study of the Holy Bible.

I am so blessed and always strive to give all situations to our Savior. I have recognized that He can handle anything and all things. He is the source of all power. My praise and honor are unto the glorious and Heavenly Father for blessing me with the wisdom and gift to compose devotionals to inspire and encourage others. God ordered my steps, and I followed. Amid it all, He placed people in my life to encourage me. Reverend Nikki Pearson suggested and encouraged me to start a blog to share my devotions with others worldwide.

I am so honored and grateful. To further encourage my scribes and growth, Pastor Billy Staton challenged me to put my devotions in a book and suggested the name Crumbs for Life. A very special thank you for the awesome artwork displayed on my cover by my son Gary Pridgeon, Jr. I know that everything is possible when God is in it. My devotional encourages me, which confirms that God is in control and I will always trust in Him.

When you allow God to use you and work your gifts, it is amazing the response you receive. I noted daily the page views, and the response gave me the incentive to really focus on messages that would attract the daily needs of everyone. I started my blog in July 2012 Expectations of God, and as of today, the stats are 13,000 page views from the following Countries:

Entry   Pageviews

Entry	Pageviews
United States	8772
Russia	978
Germany	797
France	494
Malaysia	209
Ukraine	203
Portugal	147
China	145
Poland	137
United Kingdom	84

An initial warning was given to me. Not to let my expectation of working in a Christian environment be my gauge of how things would take place or how others would behave. I have always tried to give people and circumstances the benefit of the doubt. Being opinionated by another's experience is not the key to understanding why a person is who they are. Coming to my own conclusion is justifiable by what I experienced. At the start of this new experience, I had a feeling of security. A feeling which soon was replaced with doubt and disappointment. I set my hopes on my expectations, anticipating how Christians should behave. Which, too, was an underlying judgment. Who am I to think I can point fingers or frown my face in disgust? I am still a work in progress!!

Granted, as you grow spiritually, you exercise a Christian mind set by focusing on the directives of scripture and the values implemented by your leadership. Being compelled to enforce what I knew was right, I reminded some in authority to lead by example. Was I right to criticize or reproof a person of authority?

2 Timothy 3:16-17 *All Scripture is breathed out by God and profitable for teaching, for reproof, for correction, and for training in righteousness, that the man of God may be competent, equipped for every good work.* Yet, we are instructed to respect and humble ourselves to authority. Romans 13:1-7 *Every person is to be in subjection to the governing authorities for there is no authority except from God, and those which exist are established by God. Therefore, whoever resists authority has opposed the ordinance*

of God; and they who have opposed will receive condem-
nation upon themselves. For rulers are not a cause of fear
for good behavior but for evil. Do you want to have no
fear of authority? Do what is good, and you will have
praise from the same.

Don't get me wrong, the benefits are plentiful, and there are many blessings as well. Yet, I still have the nagging in my spirit. Many times, I was afraid that the negative vibes, ungodly spirits, and falsehood would discourage me and set me back in my walk. Now, when I say set back, I don't mean returning to or pursuing things that God delivered me from. I simply mean just the behavior and character traits that had improved significantly in temperament, but not entirely. A significant number of people who know me could attest to the new changed me, the calmer me.

I know now that pursuing the Word of God, continued faith, and trust in Him kept me. Many times, I wanted just to walk away and say what I have always heard the unchurched say. A bunch of hypocrites! But again, wouldn't that be hypocrisy as well, agreeing that all Christians are hypocrites, false religious spectacles that put themselves on pedestals only to look down at the unsaved.

That I now know to be a false prejudgment from trials and experience on a personal level. By studying His Word, discipleship classes and positive experiences, I recognized that people are just people, and we need to meet them where they are. You can set the tone and be the example, or you can sound the alarm and act unwisely. A personal evaluation of your moral compass is a requirement more so than checking that of others. I know myself all too well, and surely, the first time and every time someone judges or attacks my character, the boxing match begins. Sound the alarm, ring the bell, and the mental dual begins.

Self-evaluating honestly and owning the good, the bad and the ugly. You must learn to get past what you don't like and find what you don't know, the one God wants to manifest. God can miraculously reveal things about yourself you never knew. A gift in there that surprises you is like an early birthday present. A seed that needs nourishment to develop and manifest.

It's an amazing observation of self when you recognize God's changes in your life. What is not easy is knowing those surrounding you may have a glimpse of your past or may have heard some truths, gossip, and untruths. Those who still want to hold you hostage to the very things that God has forgiven. I think some people believe that after their acceptance and salvation, they have a new birth right to judge others.

Then there are those people who look at you a certain way, as if they know what you are thinking and think they know your weaknesses. They may even anticipate your next move or say something asinine to you, like I know how you are and what you think. At the end of the day, they really want power over you. You don't understand their intentions or motives. You may ask why me? Are you that disturbed over God's creation 'the me" that I am? I challenged them to get over themselves and, while they were at it, get over me, too.

I never understood why some people think they can change who others are. Only God can change people. We must do the work to remain in His purposed will. God already knew when he created us that we would sin, could sin, and still might fall short after salvation. Temptation is the enemy's promise of temporal pleasure that comes with a free one-way ticket to hell.

Attitudes and dispositions are the results of life experiences and upbringing. You can't always understand why people negatively express themselves verbally, emotionally, or even physically unless you know their state of mind. The most important thing is how you react and respond to their actions. Only if a person shares the innermost secrets, strongholds, insecurities, and challenges will you even begin to understand the why. I say the why because only those things reveal why people think, act, and behave in the manner that they do.

I have met people who appeared to be happy, stress-free and very engaging. My first impression was based on me summarizing what I visually experienced. As time went on, at a point in the relationship, I began to see and know what was shared by the individual, the stuff. The stuff that made them tick, the stuff they found joy in, the stuff that made them crazy. The stuff that God gave them to share, to minister.

Just one day or a bad experience in a lifelong relationship can change your thoughts entirely about an individual. You can lose respect, and you may see things that you never noticed, and you may even recognize that you are so different and not understand how you ever became friends. Trust and believe that people are in our lives for reasons and seasons and some for a lifetime.

I have learned to put value in how I treat people, not how they treat me. However, I demand respect as well as I give it. Everyone is not sincere, and some have underlying motives. One thing for certain: You can't spend too much time or put a lot of energy into worrying about the behavior of others. Pray for them and keep it moving. If perhaps the things they do and say have an affect on your life, be wise and discern how to handle the relationship. You can't get and do what God has purposed you to do when you are trying to do His job.

Having transparency in how you view another alongside having no bearings of superiority when their conduct is not conducive to the environment. Now, irate, intense, disrespectful behavior can't be overlooked or dismissed. However, taking the mature approach and not feeding the demon is a wise decision. Why subject yourself to negative and demeaning energy? There are all sorts or people with all kinds of behavior and all kinds of spirits. It is up to you to be in control of your flesh. Quite often, people don't know the enemy is using them and making them act unkind and foolish.

As you recognize your core and reflect on the foundation that is being manifested in you, it is easier to dismiss the lies of the enemy. Wholeheartedly trusting God enables a broader vision. You are no longer deceived by the belief that the perception of another has a bearing on your success when God is in it. Knowing that you are the seed of Abraham "For as many of you as have been baptized into Christ have put on Christ. **Galatians 3:27-29** *There is neither Jew nor Greek, there is neither bond nor free, there is neither male nor female: for ye are all one in Christ Jesus. And if ye be Christ's, then are ye Abraham's seed, and heirs according to the promise.*".

People are going to be people wherever you go and whatever the occasion. A combination of people with a conglomerate of spirits is a mighty force to reckon with. People carry their unfavorable spirits; they go to Church, come to work, and publicly consistently drag spirits. The many negative spirits. Spirit of judgment, the spirit of deceit, the spirit of narcissism, the spirit of control, the spirit of unforgiveness, jealousy and envy, the spirit of Judas, the spirit of Jezebel, the spirit of Sanballat, the spirit of Tobias. I could go on and on, but the most important thing is to recognize the spirits you are dealing with. There may be times when you must look a demon straight in the eye and tell them that the name of Jesus has more power than anything they try to do. Pray those demonic spirits away in the matchless name of Jesus. It will depart and flee. Never be inundated with ungodly spirits and witchcraft. The victory has already been granted. **Deuteronomy 28:7**: *"The Lord will cause your enemies who rise against you to be defeated before you. They shall come out against you one way and flee before you seven ways."*

Quite often, there is a disconnect or false perception of where responsibility falls in communicating. The application of *Matthew 18:15-18 If your brother sins, go and show him his fault in private; if he listens to you, you have won your brother.*

<u>16</u> *"But if he does not listen to you, take one or two more with you, so that BY THE MOUTH OF TWO OR THREE WITNESSES EVERY FACT MAY BE CONFIRMED.*

17 *"If he refuses to listen to them, tell it to the church; and if he refuses to listen even to the church, let him be to you as a Gentile and a tax collector.*

18 *"Truly I say to you, whatever you bind on earth shall have been bound in heaven; and whatever you loose on earth shall have been loosed in heaven.* It is a Biblical principle; however, everyone doesn't follow or abide by the process. The burden of expectation is a Scriptural directive on every man, woman, or child. Therefore, regardless of your title or position, it applies to all. There are no double standards in Heaven. God's commands are not multiple-choice or for a selected group.

Scripture and my experiences have led me to understand that you must meet people where they are. I have also acknowledged that everyone is not going to like you and that you cannot change. Only God can change the heart. **Matthew 10:14** ***And whosoever shall not receive you, nor hear your words, when ye depart out of that house or city, shake off the dust of your feet.***

I am amazed at the amount of people who quote and remind you of scripture, yet they themselves do not apply these same Biblical principles. I guess maybe it is the same blind spot we suffer when giving positive advice to others. Then we do the very same thing we advise them not to do. Maybe if we all attain Biblical principles and all the positive moral and ethical standards of life, the world would be a place of excellence.

I conclude that people, their character, and their actions are merely based on choices. Your reaction more than likely is a response to an action. No one can tell anyone how to react or respond to a situation or circumstance. I wholeheartedly recognize that if you keep the peace, seek God and give circumstances and challenges to Him in His will, things will work out. It may not be the way you prefer, but it's God's plan, not yours. It is His world, and we live in it per His discretion and timing.

A great thing about working in a Christian environment is that it is an excellent teaching ground. You see the gifts of individuals manifest, and you see gifts that people have they may not recognize themselves. It is an opportunity for encouragement, evangelism, and personal growth. You may be the very person who can share a life-changing experience that provides a breakthrough for a broken being. People are hurting!!! Daily, we migrate to our workplace and may never know the pain or challenges another contends with. Unfortunately, the fear of exposure supersedes the trust. Then there are some people who share more than they should about themselves and others. I believe if a person wants to share their story, it should be their decision. Ethically, it is wrong to share with another what someone has told you in confidence. The best part of the story is not the struggle. It is the blessing of the outcome or overcome. People tend to dwell on the fall, the shortcoming or sin in the story. Spiritually, we should honor and exercise integrity when we know private and personal information. If you were not given permission to share it, then keep your peace. If an individual is delivered and freed from the experience and/or challenges, they will freely share their story with whom and when they feel led.

God has a way of placing us amidst what we need to acquire to be purposed in His plan. Personally, I had no idea that I would create a Blog Site that has over 17,000 views in countries where the Holy Bible is not allowed and Christianity is not honored. Amazing to me, but it just gives me the incentive to keep trusting, keep believing and know that God has manifested this gift in me. I ask Him to create in me a clean heart, humility, and wisdom to understand that it is all His doing and not mine. If He wants to use me, I am available. I surely admire and praise His mighty works and power.

My heart is filled with gratefulness because throughout all the good, the bad, and the ugly, I have been changed, and I am chosen. I recognize God's work. He has graced me with wisdom and discernment to see the tactics of the enemy. I see how the enemy uses good people to do his dirty work and cause you to be distracted. The devil is fully aware of the great things God has for you. So, when he can poison the thoughts of a good person with jealousy, envy, selfishness and unforgiveness to work against you, he uses them if he can. I know that the Judas spirit is real, real, real. The same people who kiss your cheek, hug you and say I love you, and I'm praying for you, maybe out to demean, deface and tarnish your character.

I had to learn to be careful when responding and reacting to the recognition of deceit in a Christian environment. Foolish me still thinking that this is so unbelievable. People who participate in Communion and the Church Covenant. Declaration led by the Spirit that we all agree with as follows:

The Baptist Covenant

Having been led, as we believe, by the Spirit of God, to receive the Lord Jesus Christ as our Savior, and on the profession of our faith, having been baptized in the name of the Father, and of the Son, and of the Holy Ghost, we do now in the presence of God, angels, and this assembly, most solemnly and joyfully enter covenant with one another as one body in Christ. We engage therefore, by the aid of the Holy Spirit to walk together in Christian love; to strive for the advancement of this church, in knowledge, holiness, and comfort; to promote its prosperity and spirituality; to sustain its worship, ordinances, discipline, and doctrines; to contribute cheerfully and regularly to the support of the ministry, the expenses of the church, the relief of the poor, and the spread of the gospel through all nations. We also engage to maintain family and secret devotion to religiously educate our children; to seek to salvation of our kindred and acquaintances; to walk circumspectly in the world; to be just in our dealings, faithful in our engagements, and exemplary in our department; to avoid all tattling, backbiting, and excessive anger; to abstain from the sale and use of intoxicating drink as a beverage, and to be zealous in our efforts to advance the kingdom of our Savior. We further engage to watch over one another in brotherly love; to remember each other in prayer; to aid each other in sickness and distress; to cultivate Christian sympathy in feeling and courtesy in speech; to be slow to take offense, but always ready for reconciliation, and mindful of the rules of our Savior, to secure it without delay. We moreover engage that, when we remove from this place, we will as soon as possible unite with some other church where we can carry out the spirit of this covenant and the principles of God's Word. And

now unto Him, who brought again from the dead our Lord
Jesus, be Power and Glory forever. Amen.

The question I ask myself is how many people read, agree, and acknowledge this declaration as a monthly routine and not a passionate proclamation in honor of the God and Father, His Son Jesus, and the Holy Spirit we proclaim and believe in. It is a demonstration of the behavior of fruitful spirits as one in Him. We only deceive ourselves and give the enemy power when we contradict in our acts the agreement of the Church. As one group in Christ, we recognize the necessity to mortify the flesh and depart from sinful ways. We fast, we pray, and we abstain from forms of immoral indulgence. Yet sinful nature remains in us if we continue to gossip, place judgment, and backbite. Quite often, Christian environments dismiss people who are faced with strongholds and hardships. They point out their sinful ways as if there is no hope, turn the cheek and do not want to be bothered. Such hypocrisy!!!!

When I hear people say that Christians are such hypocrites and that they have no desire to worship in the Church, I don't always give much thought to their opinion. I believed it to be justification for not going to Church. I personally have witnessed the hypocrisy. Nonetheless, if possible, I stepped in to do whatever I could to rectify the treatment of unworthiness or unimportance. Some people think it is a Christian right to choose whom Salvation and ministering should be offered.

1 Corinthians 1:27 - 28 *God hath chosen the weak things*
of the world to confound the things which are mighty.
God chose the lowly things of this world and the despised

things--and the things that are not--to nullify the things that are.

Hurt people hurt others, and many suffer deep-rooted issues that have become dormant in their spirit. In the face of sin, some people see their past mistakes and perhaps have not forgiven themselves. In their fragility and vulnerability, they choose not to minister to an individual. Such behavior causes bitterness and resentment for the Church. A place where encouragement, inspiration and prayer should be a priority.

We all have issues; until we face our demons and forgive ourselves, we can't effectively fulfill our purpose. I believe you can still operate in your gift but are not giving the best of yourself. **Romans 3:23 – 24 *For all have sinned and come short of the glory of God; 24 Being justified freely by his grace through the redemption that is in Christ Jesus:*** If you know that God has called you to Ministry, as you study His Word clearly you know that you are held at a higher calling and expectation. **Titus 1:7-9 *For the overseer must be above reproach as God's steward, not self-willed, not quick-tempered, not addicted to wine, not pugnacious, not fond of sordid gain, but hospitable, loving what is good, sensible, just, devout, self-controlled, holding fast the faithful word which is in accordance with the teaching, so that he will be able both to exhort in sound doctrine and to refute those who contradict.*** Know the voice and directives God has placed on your life.

Malicious people throw shade, make accusations, be dishonest and demonstrate foul behavior. When you call them on their messiness, the same people claim victimization, finding all sorts of justifications other than owning it. I have, through growth, acquired the ability not to allow their twisted, stinking thinking to funk up my personal space. I clearly recognize that I am not immune to enemy attacks, and the same applies to those people that the enemy uses. He penetrates them with ill thoughts and behavior because they allow it—a lack of spiritual growth.

Know that God's wrath is coming for the judgmental, prideful, and self-centered. Knowledge of this helps to move past the messiness. Vengeance is not yours, and it belongs to God. No one wants to be bothered with foolishness. Therefore, you limit your interaction with them to a professional level only. Unfortunately, these same people who caused you to disengage on a personal level expect you to be engaged in conversation and activity with them. It amazes me how people will imply that something is wrong with you, yet your disconnect is a response to how they treated you. As well as the treatment you have witnessed others experience.

You would expect people to be honorable and speak the truth in a Christian environment. However, I can attest to the black balling of one's character. If you are a person who will speak up or defend your rights, your character is attacked. Many support their judgment of others in the book Spirit Controlled Temperament, written by Tim La Haye, as a prescribed regimen. Brainwashing can be very dangerous. Some people find credibility in horoscopes which is another depiction of character traits. None of these studies or illustrations of character are based on scripture, so I find it not to be full proof. That's my opinion, and I'm sticking with it. Anybody can be any temperament on the right or wrong day, depending on the circumstance and culture.

Sometimes, we place too many layers on simple things. My father has always told me there are two ways in life: right and wrong. So basically, in the spiritual realm, are you speaking or doing things outside of the directives of God? Is your behavior conducive to the Fruits of the Spirit? Now, that is a firm trajectory of righteousness.

Working in a Christian establishment has been a hands-on training in behavioral science. God has opened my eyes wider and poured so much more wisdom into me. We tend to spend more time and energy pointing fingers and finding fault in another versus self-examination. Who are you in the eyes of God? Are you living according to His Word? We all have much work to be done. If every time we attempt to attack or pick someone apart, then use those same building blocks we are shifting to build them up, we then are evangelizing them as well as ourselves. If you see a lack and don't encourage the individual, you are also lacking. **Matthew 7:1-2** *"Do not judge, or you too will be judged. 2 For in the same way you judge others, you will be judged, and with the measure you use, it will be measured to you.*

When you check yourself and find ways and thoughts that shouldn't be, the cleanup and purging should begin, and correction should never end. There is always something that you can change to be a better you. God already knew we'd be extra in our frailty. God knew we would need a Savior to rescue us from our flesh and troubled minds. I believe we all suffer with battles of the mind. The devil is a beast, and if he can penetrate your thoughts, he can alter your behavior.

Recognizing the fact that the Church is a hospital for the sick, not just the unhealthy, confused mind or hopeless in need of prayer and encouragement, but the spiritually ill. A person usually doesn't know they have a tumor or abnormal growth in their body until the doctor diagnoses the systems and gets the results from testing. God has a way of revealing your spiritual diseases by exposing the signs. Sometimes, those diseases are deep-rooted and need extraction, like a decayed tooth. A dentist will prepare and numb the gum areas surrounding the bad tooth. God may use circumstances and people to prepare you for a diagnosis of your unforgiveness, selfishness, pride fullness and any other unhealthy condition you may have. After which, He will give you confirmation. **Isaiah 18:5 *For before the harvest, as soon as the bud blossoms and the flower becomes a ripening grape, Then He will cut off the sprigs with pruning knives and remove and cut away the spreading branches.***

I acknowledge that nothing is, perhaps, and everything serves a purpose. Every challenge and circumstance I have faced was missioned by God. God places a course for conduct in our pathway. It is important that we make the right choices. You will live with the choices you make. The right way or wrong way option lies before us in all situations. I find that quite often, the hardest choices are the right choices. The drawing of the flesh and desire to be right, aside from leaning to our own understanding, causes us to make wrong decisions. Seeking God is key, and knowing His voice. He will direct your path. We tend to make a mess out of things and then seek His grace to fix it. **Proverbs 3:5-6 5** *Trust in the Lord with all your heart and lean not on your own understanding; 6 in all your ways submit to him, and he will make your paths straight.*

In terms of accountability, everyone needs someone in their life that will hold them accountable. However, everyone who avails themselves of mentorship is not qualified. A thorough observation of how they live and treat others, alongside prayer and direction from God, is needed when choosing a mentor. Not all leaders are candidates. As I mentioned earlier, people in leadership should lead by example. You can learn something from a bad leader. My father always told me you can learn something from a fool. If an individual is knowledgeable in areas spiritually or professionally where you need growth, those are the things you can value and learn from them. **Proverbs 27:17** *Iron sharpeneth iron; so a man sharpeneth the countenance of his friend.* The essential point is that all, as in everybody, should be held accountable to Scripture, the ministry's passion, and the Church's core values. I believe that we should practice what we preach.

Be accountable to God first. Aside from being accountable to a mentor or leader, be accountable to yourself. When you know right from wrong and apply Biblical principles, doing the right things becomes second nature. Christian behavior is instinctive if you live according to God's commands and expectations. Knowing and doing are two different things. Be responsible for your actions, your thoughts, and the things you say to others. You know when you are outside of the realms of kindness and wisdom. God sees all, knows all and hears every spoken word. Some people would rather operate in a lie than act on what is true. What I do know is that knowing the truth, being honest, and operating in truth gives you freedom and peace in your spirit. The best thing you can do for yourself is to own your stuff. Accepting who you are, your flaws and your mistakes makes it easier to receive reproofing and directives. Too often, people don't practice and operate truthfully, but they expect you to do so. If you tell me what God is expecting and the things that are pleasing in His sight, practice what you preach. Righteousness is not provisional. Moral law and values apply to everyone, regardless of your position or title.

As we all know, anyone can slip at any time because we are all human and flesh-driven. We must let the Holy Spirit do the driving and suppress our fleshly responses and actions. Unfortunately, when people are not held accountable, their slips fall. These falls become habit and character defects. I conclude that at the end of the day, everything and everyone must be responsible for the decisions and choices they make. Clean up your act and stop trying to point out the flaws of others. Self-righteousness falls in line with pride, and neither is pleasing in the sight of God. God will do the judging, and God will do the correcting. Judgment is out of our hands. When people start trying to do God's work, they are setting themselves up for His wrath. Stay in your lane. Learn to pray for others and their sinful ways.

Transforming God's Word and power in our lives doesn't just happen; we must do the work. God so willingly gives us what we need. Faithfully trust in Him. Saying you trust God but then dipping your mouth and hands into what you said you gave to him is not 100% trust. Who can you trust your all to

100%? Not one individual...God and God only. Faith and trust in God prepare us for His purpose. As we build a relationship with God, we know His voice, and He'll direct our path and give us peace. **Romans 15:13** *13 Now may the God of hope fill you with all joy and peace in believing, that you may abound in hope by the power of the Holy Spirit.*

I would like to share some of the most viewed crumbs of my blog, "Expectation of God." I pray that in viewing these blogs, you will find many take-a-ways and find the referenced scripture as an application to life challenges you may face.

The Church

Many Christians attending Church will tell non-Christians they need to attend Church. Some people were never exposed as a child, and many, out of ignorance, don't attend. I heard people say that people in the Church are a bunch of hypocrites. There are so many reasons and excuses why many do not attend Church.

I think the stance and focus as a Christian should be deliberate when representing the Church; we are the Church and should live according to the commands and expectations of God. People should be able to distinguish who we are by our character traits and behavior outside of the Church dwelling.

Although there are no perfect people if you are called to a ministry and you answer the call. One should walk in their position. A Pastor, Reverend, Minister and a man or woman of God should stand out in the example of God's Word. To be respected and in a position to mentor and minister, you should be the Church God has placed in you.

Attending Church is important; however, the Church is the people, not the building.

LACOUNTESS B. CORBITT

Romans 12:4-5 (NKJV)

For as we have many members in one body, but all the members do not have the same function, [5] so we, being many, are one body in Christ, and individually members of one another. Always be reminded of who and what you represent. Be the Church!!!

Corinthians 1:2 (NKJV)

To the church of God which is at Corinth, to those who are sanctified in Christ Jesus, called to be saints, with all who in every place call on the name of Jesus Christ our Lord, both theirs and ours:

Acts 20:28 (KJV)

Take heed therefore unto yourselves, and to all the flock, over the which the Holy Ghost hath made you overseers, to feed the church of God, which he hath purchased with his own blood.

Colossians 3:16 (KJV)

Let the word of Christ dwell in you richly in all wisdom; teaching and admonishing one another in psalms and hymns and spiritual songs, singing with grace in your hearts to the Lord.

Like A Quiet Storm

A storm normally would be translated by a severe disturbance of the atmosphere consisting of some or all elements such as rain, wind, hail, sleet, and snow. The heavy onset of a severe storm can impact the lives of many by preventing the normal flow of things.

We sometimes in life experience a sudden or violent commotion that causes an emotional storm. The sequence of challenging events and circumstances is most often out of our control. Faith is a strong belief largely based on apprehension rather than proof. It is the unwavering trust we have in God. God's ability to bless and extend grace and mercy at any given time is like a quiet storm.

Just as God controls the earth, the change of seasons, God can literally instantaneously change your life and circumstances in the blink of an eye. His power supersedes and controls all storms. Although a storm can and may cause devastation, know that God is still in control.

Matthew 7:24-27

"Therefore, everyone who hears these words of Mine and acts on them, may be compared to a wise man who built his house on the rock. "And the rain fell, and the floods came, and the winds blew and slammed against that house; and yet it did not fall, for it had been founded on the rock. "Everyone who hears these words of Mine and does not act on them, will be like a foolish man who built his house on the sand.

Psalm 107:29

He caused the storm to be still, So that the waves of the sea were hushed.

Luke 8:24

They came to Jesus and woke Him up, saying, "Master, Master, we are perishing!" And He got up and rebuked the wind and the surging waves, and they stopped, and it became calm.

Toxic Behavior

We may encounter or witness someone demonstrating negativity in their behavior or spoken words daily. When individuals act in an undesirable manner, they are allowing the enemy to use them. Too often, we fall into the trap of responding to negativity with negativity versus positive responses, counteracting and reducing the forces of evil.

Christian character and moral qualities will be challenged. The enemy knows the positive traits and expectations of God. It is his goal to demolish righteous and upstanding qualities. The truth is that God has provided us with the tools needed to defeat enemy attacks. No evil overpowers the Word of God. It is our faith and trust in God and His Word that wins no matter how dim the situation appears to be.

2 Corinthians 10:4-6

4 For the weapons of our warfare are not carnal but mighty in God for pulling down strongholds,

5 casting down arguments and every high thing that exalts itself against the knowledge of God, bringing every thought into captivity to the obedience of Christ,

6 and being ready to punish all disobedience when your obedience is fulfilled. As we understand that forces are beyond us we then realize that without God we are hopeless in battle.

Incorporate God in our lives daily, trust Him in all things and all ways, putting on the full armor without delay and distraction. He knows every struggle and every attack. With Him in Him no weapon formed against us shall prosper.

2 Corinthians 10:34

For though we walk in the flesh, we do not war according to the flesh, for the weapons of our warfare are not of the flesh, but divinely powerful for the destruction of fortresses.

1 Peter 4:12-13

Beloved, do not be surprised at the fiery ordeal among you, which comes upon you for your testing, as though some strange thing were happening to you; but to the degree that you share the sufferings of Christ, keep on rejoicing, so that also at the revelation of His glory you may rejoice with exultation.

Ephesians 6:11-17 (NKJV)

11 Put on the whole armor of God, that you may be able to stand against the wiles of the devil.

12 For we do not wrestle against flesh and blood, but against principalities, against powers, against the rulers of the darkness of this age, against spiritual hosts of wickedness in the heavenly places.

13 Therefore take up the whole armor of God, that you may be able to withstand in the evil day, and having done all, to stand.

14 Stand therefore, having girded your waist with truth, having put on the breastplate of righteousness,

15 and having shod your feet with the preparation of the gospel of peace;

16 above all, taking the shield of faith with which you will be able to quench all the fiery darts of the wicked one

17 And take the helmet of salvation, and the sword of the Spirit, which is the word of God;

In the Mirror

A s we gaze at ourselves in the mirror, we see an image of what we look like to others. We can change our expressions and appearance. Women can add highlights of makeup, and men can either allow facial hair to grow or shave. People are identified by their facial features.

It would be amazing and less complicated if we could identify a person by the meditations of their heart. If we knew what another was feeling within or had a visual of their emotions, we would be mindful and less likely to engage with some people.

God has the wisdom and understanding and knows that giving us these abilities would hinder our abilities and growth.

Knowing that others can't see our hearts, we can mask our feelings and emotions alongside ill intentions. We may be able to fool some people sometimes, but God knows just what we don't want others to see or know. God sees everything and knows all about all mankind. No one escapes his judgment.

Blessed are the pure at heart. If your heart is not clear and you are holding onto anger, bitterness, unforgiveness, greed, and deceit, you will not enter the Kingdom of God. Ask God to purge and cleanse your ailing heart of all the things that are not pleasing in his sight. A renewed spirit restored peace, and joy of The Lord will be the reflection coming from your heart.

Matthew 5:8 ESV

"Blessed are the pure in heart, for they shall see God.

Psalm 51:10 ESV

Create in me a clean heart, O God, and renew a right spirit within me.

2 Timothy 2:22 ESV

So, flee youthful passions and pursue righteousness, faith, love, and peace, along with those who call on the Lord from a pure heart.

Hebrews 10:22 ESV

Let us draw near with a true heart in full assurance of faith, with our hearts sprinkled clean from an evil conscience and our bodies washed with pure water.

Listening or Hearing

It amazes me how music has changed. I remember listening to music and enjoying not only the sound but the lyrics as well. We knew most songs lyric by lyric entirely. We listened to the music and heard and related to ourselves or others. Sometimes, the lyrics could be personalized to our lifestyles or the way we approach situations.

Do you listen to the Word of God, or are you hearing Him in His structuring of character and lifestyle? Many of us can quote scripture or make suggestions to others when needed, but do you live the things you preach? For years, I listened to what was being preached and clearly understood what God ordained and decreed, but I was not hearing it.

The greatest part of knowing, listening, and hearing God's Word is when you see the blessings of application. Exercising and executing God's will and plans opens your eyes to see and heart to receive the blessings purposed for you and your life.

Romans 10:17 (NKJV)

17 So then faith comes by hearing and hearing by the word of God.

Revelation 3:22 (NKJV)

22 "He who has an ear, let him hear what the Spirit says to the churches."

Psalm 1:1-2 (NIV)

1 Blessed is the one who does not walk in step with the wicked or stand in the way that sinners take or sit in the company of mockers,

2 but whose delight is in the law of the Lord, and who meditates on his law day and night.

Just Too Much

Our personal and present circumstances at times can be difficult, promoting overwhelming emotions. Once we are overwhelmed with negative emotions, our actions and character may to others appear to be out of context. Many times, we display anger, bitterness, hate and sadness. All of which is what we feel and is humanly natural.

The great thing about trusting God is when things become too much to handle. He can give you peace. When we believe God's Word and His promises, we understand that He works all things out for the good of His purpose during those down times. Trust God if what you are going through is just too much.

God is a Healer, a Provider, a Counselor, a Peacemaker, and He can do all things. There is nothing too hard for God. His Omnipotence and Omnipresence are beyond human conception. However, it is real, perfect, and true. Your power is only the power He has bestowed and portioned in you. Your limitations do not dictate your trust in Him. When things are just too much trust the Creator and God that has ALL POWER.

Ephesians 1:19 (NKJV)

19 and what is the exceeding greatness of His power toward us who believe, according to the working of His mighty power

Psalm 139:7-10 (NKJV)

7 Where can I go from Your Spirit? Or where can I flee from Your presence?

8 If I ascend into heaven, You are there; If I make my bed in hell, behold, You are there.

9 If I take the wings of the morning, And dwell in the uttermost parts of the sea,

10 Even there Your hand shall lead me, And Your right hand shall hold me.

Proverbs 15:3 (NKJV)

The eyes of the Lord are in every place, Keeping watch on the evil and the good.

You Want More

There are so many aspirations we pray for, wish for and ask God to fulfill. The unfulfilled desires can often hinder our emotions, causing envy of others. God does not intend to cause envy or jealousy among His children. He has purposely designed a plan for each life according to His will.

Unfortunately, people want more than what God has planned for their life. What God has for you is for you. Sometimes, we pay too close attention to what others have, which blinds our vision, and we don't appreciate what God has blessed us with. Do not covet the possessions of others or things that are temporal.

Let your thirst and hunger be for a relationship with God. God promised that He will provide for your needs and trust that His abilities are immeasurable. If it is His Will He can do more than you could ask or imagine. Just keep faith in Him; when God says no, He knows what is best for you.

Philippians 4:19 (NW)

And my God shall supply all your need according to His riches in glory by Christ Jesus.

Ephesians 3:20 (NKJV)

Now to Him who is able to do exceedingly abundantly above all that we ask or think, according to the power that works in us,

James 3:16 (NW)

16 For where envy and self-seeking exist, confusion and every evil thing are there.

Evicted

E viction often weighs harshly on the parties involved if the circumstances are out of their control. It simply happens when a property owner evicts a tenant after they have not paid the rent.

Sadly, people allow the enemy to lay up in their houses without paying a dime. He has never paid anyone for housing him. He just roams from place to place and from situation to situation. A true freeloader and possessor of havoc. If he's lodging in your home, you need to force him out and off your property. Serve him eviction immediately!!!

Jesus paid ransom, and He paid a cost that we could never repay. He should be the only one resting and residing in your home. The great thing about it is that He continues to give and fulfill the promises of the Father. He is a Healer, Protector, Burden Bearer, Light of the World, He is the Truth, He is Love.

Beyond all the spectacular gifts He gives, He has prepared a place for us to spend our lives eternally. He has a place for all who believe in Heaven in a Mansion with He and the Father. He is forever welcome in my home.

John 10:10 (NKJV)

10 The thief does not come except to steal, and to kill, and to destroy. I have come that they may have life, and that they may have it more abundantly.

John 14:3 (NKJV)

3 And if I go and prepare a place for you, I will come again and receive you to Myself; that where I am, there you may be also.

Romans 3:23-24 (NKJV)

23 for all have sinned and fall short of the glory of God,

24 being justified freely by His grace through the redemption that is in Christ Jesus,

Can Take the I'm Out

In many situations and circumstances, my carnal mind immediately fed on the thoughts of failure. Yet many times, things turned around for me, and the situation became a blessing and memory. Sometimes, we don't recognize the favor of God in our circumstances. He can and will work things out if it is His will.

Spiritual growth and wisdom have broadened my vision in life. God's Word gives you an insight into God's greatness and unlimited abilities. I now recognize that a situation may not be filtered out according to my desires, but all things work together for the good of Him.

God can do anything God wants to do. He has all the power and control over every situation and everyone. Trust and have faith in the source of all power. God can take the (I'm) out of the impossible. So, through Him, all things are possible!!!!

Ephesians 3:20 (NKJV)

20 Now unto Him who is able to do exceedingly abundantly above all that we ask or think, according to the power that works in us,

Mark 10:27 (NKJV)

27 But Jesus looked at them and said, "With men it is impossible, but not with God; for with God all things are possible."

Philippians 4:13 (NKJV)

13 I can do all things through Christ who strengthens me.

Unnoticed

C hildren look forward to their parent's acknowledgment of a positive accomplishment. They love the attention and praise. Not only do children like to be noticed for their achievements, but adults do as well. Some people go out of their way to be noticed. On the other hand, no one strives for recognition of notoriety.

Although no mention is made in many circumstances, everything we do and everything we say is noticed by someone. You may recognize that some people always recognize and respond to you making a mistake. Yet these same people never have anything positive to say when you achieve a planned objective.

Do not allow the contemptuous characterization of others to be your affirmation. Know that God sees everything we do and hears every spoken word. We should allow God to be the source of empowerment we gauge ourselves by. Trust in His Word and promises, allowing Him to direct your path. He is the source of your being and the only one who has the right to judge your life. You are always noticed.

Job 34:21-22

"For His eyes are upon the ways of a man, And He sees all his steps. "There is no darkness or deep shadow Where the workers of iniquity may hide themselves.

Jeremiah 17:10

"I, the LORD, search the heart, I test the mind, Even to give to each man according to his ways, According to the results of his deeds.

Job 22:13-14

"You say, 'What does God know? Can He judge through the thick darkness? 'Clouds are a hiding place for Him, so that He cannot see; And He walks on the vault of heaven.'

Psalm 94:9-11

He who planted the ear, does He not hear? He who formed the eye, does He not see? He who chastens the nations, will He not rebuke, Even He who teaches man knowledge? The LORD knows the thoughts of man, That they are a mere breath.

Can God Use Me

The thoughts of your past haunt you and hold you hostage. As you glance at the reflection of who you were, try to focus in on how you have changed. Yet you cannot imagine that God can use you.

Despite all the wrong choices and displeasing behavior you once displayed. God has an intended purpose for you; yes, He can use you. In fact, He can turn your mess into a message. Some of the things we may be ashamed of are the very things that made you strong.

Job 42:2 (NKJV)

2 "I know that You can do everything, And that no purpose of Yours can be withheld from You.

So, as you dig down and reach back into your sin, focus on the lesson you learned, the story you can share, and embrace the moment of reflection. Use it as an opportunity to give testimony. A lifestyle that could have killed you now offers a future.

As you progress in you walk with God allow Him to manifest in you the purposed plan. Trust and know that God can and will use you for His Glory.

Ephesians 2:1 (NKJV)

He made alive, who were dead in trespasses and sins,

Romans 12:4-8 (NW)

4 For as we have many members in one body, but all the members do not have the same function,

5 so we, being many, are one body in Christ, and individually members of one another.

6 Having then gifts differing according to the grace that is given to us, let us use them: if prophecy, let us prophesy in proportion to our faith;

7 or ministry, let us use it in our ministering; he who teaches, in teaching;

8 he who exhorts, in exhortation; he who gives, with liberality; he who leads, with diligence; he who shows mercy, with cheerfulness

Job 42:2 (NKJV)

"I know that You can do everything, And that no purpose of Yours can be withheld from You.

Faultfinder

In your Christian walk, you may encounter those who are judgmental and find reason to criticize others either by their opinion or facts that relate to your past.

Romans 2:1-3 (NKJV)

1 Therefore you are inexcusable, O man, whoever you are who judge, for in whatever you judge another you condemn yourself; for you who judge practice the same things.

2 But we know that the judgment of God is according to truth against those who practice such things.

3 And do you think this, O man, you who judge those practicing such things, and doing the same, that you will escape the judgment of God? Unfortunately, the narrow-minded listen to the harmful statements and you then have a reputation based on the implications of a critic.

Don't have the expectation that other Christians won't hold on to your past sin. They will defame and smear your story, some intentionally and some unintentionally. Let them talk!!! GOD knows all about your struggle, and this smearing of your character means nothing in the eyes of God. He has forgiven you of your sins.

Focus and interact with those who commend your growth and esteem you, respecting the change in you. God will lead and guide your footsteps to walk through circumstances and hurdle every storm. God can move any mountain and obstacle the enemy sends your way. Trust God and know that He will open doors beyond your imagination.

Luke 6:37 (NKJV)

37 "Judge not, and you shall not be judged. Condemn not, and you shall not be condemned. Forgive, and you will be forgiven.

Romans 14:12-13 (NKJV)

12 So then each of us shall give account of himself to God.

13 Therefore let us not judge one another anymore, but rather resolve this, not to put a stumbling block or a cause to fall in our brother's way.

James 4:11-12 (NKJV)

11 Do not speak evil of one another, brethren. He who speaks evil of a brother and judges his brother, speaks evil of the law and judges the law. But if you judge the law, you are not a doer of the law but a judge.

12 There is one Lawgiver, who is able to save and to destroy. Who[b] are you to judge another?

Grieved

No one can predetermine the effect a loss of a loved one will have on them. There is no scale to predict the effect according to the relationship. We all will suffer and endure the pain of losing a loved one. It is also possible to feel the pain of another as they suffer a loss.

Some may endure great sorrow and distress that lingers for long periods of time, which may require counseling/ ministering. I believe the greater your relationship with God and understanding His plan for humanity, the less anguished you will be. I remember a quote "Everybody wants to go to Heaven, but nobody wants to die".

1 Thessalonians 4:13-18

13 But I do not want you to be ignorant, brethren, concerning those who have fallen asleep, lest you sorrow as others who have no hope.

14 For if we believe that Jesus died and rose again, even so God will bring with Him those who sleep in Jesus.

15 For this we say to you by the word of the Lord, that we who are alive and remain until the coming of the Lord will by no means precede those who are asleep.

16 For the Lord Himself will descend from heaven with a shout, with the voice of an archangel, and with the trumpet of God. And the dead in Christ will rise first.

17 Then we who are alive and remain shall be caught up together with them in the clouds to meet the Lord in the air. And thus we shall always be with the Lord.

18 Therefore comfort one another with these words.

It is amazing that we desire to stay on earth knowing God has a perfect and immaculate place in glory called Heaven. Perhaps you have suffered a great loss trust in God and know that this is all part of His Master Plan.

Matthew 5:4 (NKJV)

4 Blessed are those who mourn, For they shall be comforted.

Revelation 21:4 (NKJV)

4 And God will wipe away every tear from their eyes; there shall be no more death, nor sorrow, nor crying. There shall be no more pain, for the former things have passed away."

Psalm 23:4 (NKJV)

Yea, though I walk through the valley of the shadow of death, I will fear no evil; For You are with me; Your rod and Your staff, they comfort me.

Credibility

D espite one's title or position, they may need to prove their credibility. Some people have the expertise and skill to inspire belief to obtain the position, yet they are not worthy of trust. Their power to elicit belief is intentionally used to mislead.

A Christian should be a person of integrity and trustworthiness. Unfortunately, that is not always the case.

Ephesians 4:25 (NKJV)

25 Therefore, putting away lying, "Let each one of you speak truth with his neighbor," for we are members of one another. People that are not credible usually manipulate situations and circumstances to benefit a personal desire or need to satisfy someone else that offers favor. Anything gained under false pretense is not a blessing.

God is truth, and to please Him, we must live upstanding and honest lives.

Numbers 23:19 (NKJV)

19 "God is not a man, that He should lie, Nor a son of man, that He should repent. Has He said, and will He not do? Or has He spoken, and will He not make it good? We must recognize that there are people that live a lie and need prayer. Ask God to open their eyes to see that He is truth and that honesty and credibility are important characteristics a Christian must share.

John 17:17 (NKJV)

17 Sanctify them by Your truth. Your word is truth.

Psalm 43:3 (NKJV)

3 Oh, send out Your light and Your truth! Let them lead me; Let them bring me to Your holy hill And to Your tabernacle.

John 8:31-32 (NKJV)

31 Then Jesus said to those Jews who believed Him, "If you abide in My word, you are My disciples indeed.

32 And you shall know the truth, and the truth shall make you free."

Identity Theft

Fifteen million victims suffer yearly from identity theft. This is a fast-growing crime, and statistics show that it amounts to over $50 billion in damages. Be alarmed and aware because these fraudsters are getting wiser and have more tools available to utilize when stealing personal identities.

These fraudsters are by no means as sneaky and conniving as the enemy himself. He has manipulated and tormented your mind in many ways. You are angry, bitter, hateful, and mean. Some days, you are intoxicated, and most of the time, you speak to others in an unkind way. You're not a friendly person, and you spitefully do and say things to hurt others. Most often, you do things and don't even understand or know why you behaved that way.

How great would the statistics be if a census were taken on the number of people who have allowed the enemy to steal their identity? If you are living according to your will in the flesh, your identity has been stolen. You have allowed the enemy to work through you. You are not the person God has planned for you to be. You have a purpose. Don't let the devil steal your destiny. For you is a gift of God.

Luke 22:31-32 (NKJV)

31 And the Lord said, "Simon, Simon! Indeed, Satan has asked for you, that he may sift you as wheat.

32 But I have prayed for you, that your faith should not fail; and when you have returned to Me, strengthen your brethren."

Ephesians 4:23-32 (NKJV)

23 and be renewed in the spirit of your mind,

24 and that you put on the new man which was created according to God, in true righteousness and holiness.

25 Therefore, putting away lying, "Let each one of you speak truth with his neighbor," for we are members of one another.

26 "Be angry, and do not sin": do not let the sun go down on your wrath,

27 nor give place to the devil.

28 Let him who stole steal no longer, but rather let him labor, working with his hands what is good, that he may have something to give him who has need.

29 Let no corrupt word proceed out of your mouth, but what is good for necessary edification, that it may impart grace to the hearers.

30 And do not grieve the Holy Spirit of God, by whom you were sealed for the day of redemption.

31 Let all bitterness, wrath, anger, clamor, and evil speaking be put away from you, with all malice. 32 And be kind to one another, tenderhearted, forgiving one another, even as God in Christ forgave you.

Heavenly Vested

M any people sacrifice years of service on a job that they really don't like. To receive the right to be vested in an employee pension plan, employee benefit, stock option, or profit-sharing retirement benefit plan, you will have to serve the required time.

How much time and interest do you invest in being Heavenly vested? When life ends, the eternal retirement plan is the most important investment. The great thing about this plan is that you don't have to pay for it. It was paid in full. Jesus paid the cost and vested the time.

God laid out a plan and gave specific details and instructions in His Word. The full package is offered in The Holy Bible. Get started today being Heavenly vested.

John 5:24 (NKJV)

24 "Most assuredly, I say to you, he who hears My word and believes in Him who sent Me has everlasting life, and shall not come into judgment, but has passed from death into life.

1 Corinthians 2:9 (NKJV)

9 But as it is written: Eye has not seen, nor ear heard, Nor have entered into the heart of man The things which God has prepared for those who love Him."

John 6:50-51 (NKJV)

50 This is the bread which comes down from heaven that one may eat of it and not die.

51 I am the living bread which came down from heaven. If anyone eats of this bread, he will live forever; and the bread that I shall give is My flesh, which I shall give for the life of the world."

Slipped on One

A mazingly, people feel justified and in good standing when they fail to be obedient if they are only falling short of one commandment. The Word of God clearly stipulates the desires of God and the things that are required to be a Christian in good standing. There are no loopholes. All may fall short at one time, but consistently is a problem.

2 Timothy 3: 16-17 (NKJV)

16 All Scripture is given by inspiration of God, and is profitable for doctrine, for reproof, for correction, for instruction in righteousness,

17 that the man of God may be complete, thoroughly equipped for every good work.

Most of the sins that people proclaim that they slipped on are ones they never let go of. God didn't say you can slide on that one sin you can't let go of. If you are continuously slipping on one sin, isn't it possible for you to slip on two, then maybe three. Your mind must be renewed.

1 Corinthians 6:9-10 (NKJV)

9 Do you not know that the unrighteous will not inherit the kingdom of God? Do not be deceived. Neither fornicators, nor idolaters, nor adulterers, nor homosexuals, nor sodomites,

10 nor thieves, nor covetous, nor drunkards, nor revilers, nor extortioners will inherit the kingdom of God.

Once you totally surrender and allow God to purge and change you the thought of going back to who you were will vex your spirit. There is no reward for minimized sin or just slipping on one sin. Gods commands are not multiple choice. The only full proof way to please God is to live according to His commandments allowing Him to renew your mind and cleanse you from all strongholds and weaknesses. Only God can deliver you from that one sin you continue to slip on.

1 Peter 2:9 (NKJV)

9 But you are a chosen generation, a royal priesthood, a holy nation, His own special people, that you may proclaim the praises of Him who called you out of darkness into His marvelous light;

Romans 6:14-16 (NKJV)

14 For sin shall not have dominion over you, for you are not under law but under grace.

15 What then? Shall we sin because we are not under law but under grace? Certainly not!

16 Do you not know that to whom you present yourselves slaves to obey, you are that one's slaves whom you

Galatians 5:6 (NKJV)

6 Stand fast therefore in the liberty by which Christ has made us free, and do not be entangled again with a yoke of bondage.

Keeping Promises

I t is a normal expectation that when someone makes a promise, they do what they promised. It is so important to be a person of your word. People may not take you seriously or respect your word when you do not bond to it.

Although we expect a person to be forthcoming with a promise, God instructed in His Word to place our faith in Him not man.

2 Corinthians 1:20 (NKJV)

20 For all the promises of God in Him are Yes, and in Him Amen, to the glory of God through us. Perhaps our disappointments will not be as devastating and personal if we practice that command.

The only full proof promises are from God, our Creator whose Word is Truth. You can faithfully trust and believe the promises of God. God promised that He inspires all Scriptures in the Bible. We therefore can be assured that everything revealed and learned in the Bible came from God.

2 Timothy 3:16-17 (NKJV)

16 All Scripture is given by inspiration of God, and is profitable for doctrine, for reproof, for correction, for instruction in right-eousness,

17 that the man of God may be complete, thoroughly equipped for every good work.

Titus 1:2 (NKJV)

2 In hope of eternal life which God, who cannot lie, promised before time began,

Genesis 28:15 (NKJV)

15 Behold, I am with you and will keep you wherever you go and will bring you back to this land; for I will not leave you until I have done what I have spoken to you."

Numbers 23:19 (NW)

19 "God is not a man, that He should lie, Nor a son of man, that He should repent. Has He said, and will He not do? Or has He spoken, and will He not make it good?

Watch Your Mouth

P eriodically, you may be involved in a conversation that soon becomes gossip. You never intended for the conversation to take the turn that it did, but you found yourself agreeing and commenting on an issue that you should not. We must learn to listen more and talk less.

James 1:19-20 (NKJV)

19 So then, my beloved brethren, let every man be swift to hear, slow to speak, slow to wrath;

20 for the wrath of man does not produce the righteousness of God.

You cannot control what others talk about or their comments, but you are in total control of what conversations you get involved in and the words you speak. Always think before you speak and ask yourself if you are thinking kind, encouraging words to speak. Would God be disappointed in my thoughts and spoken words? An old cliché is if you don't have anything nice to say, then don't say anything at all.

Psalm 19:14 (NKJV)

14 Let the words of my mouth and the meditation of my heart be acceptable in Your sight, O Lord, my strength, and my Redeemer.

Self-examination will reveal the frequency and sources whereby you fall short and are involved in conversations unfavorable to others and your character. Ask God to help you grow spiritually in this area and to give you wisdom to know when to avoid situations where you will need to watch your mouth.

Proverbs 15:2 (NKJV)

2 The tongue of the wise uses knowledge rightly

Proverbs 31:26 (NKJV)

26 She opens her mouth with wisdom, And on her tongue [is] the law of kindness.

Psalm 34: 13 (NKJV)

13 Keep your tongue from evil, And your lips from speaking deceit.

Values

Most people like the finer things in life. We tend to place value on our possessions. Often, we place a higher value on personal things than their actual worth. It may be sentimental reasons or just personal favor for the object.

Expensive cars depreciate when you drive away from the dealer immediately after purchasing. Home values have certainly decreased value in the last five to eight years. I was taught in an Accounting class that our assets equal our liabilities plus our proprietorship (basically what you owe, what you own and what you are worth). That sounds great; the downside of this is that we can't take any of those material things with us, and they have no value in God's Kingdom.

Matthew 16:26 (NKJV)

26 for what profit is it to a man if he gains the whole world, and loses his own soul? Or what will a man give in exchange for his soul?

With that in mind, we need to reexamine ourselves and restructure our focus and our personal values. After several losses, I recaptured my inner self from the pity party I was in, and I placed my value and faith in things eternal. One of my favorite sayings is that you will never see a U-Haul or Brinks following a hearse. So, I challenge you to reevaluate your desires to love stuff and remember, don't love things that cannot love you back!!!

1 Peter 1:18-20 (NKJV)

18 knowing that you were not redeemed with corruptible things, like silver or gold, from your aimless conduct received by tradition from your fathers,

19 but with the precious blood of Christ, as of a lamb without blemish and without spot.

1 Timothy 6:9-10 (NKJV)

9 But those who desire to be rich fall into temptation and a snare, and into many foolish and harmful lusts which drown men in destruction and perdition.

10 For the love of money is a root of all kinds of evil, for which some have strayed from the faith in their greediness, and pierced themselves through with many sorrows.

Matthew 6:33 (NKJV)

33 but seek first the kingdom of God and His righteousness, and all these things shall be added to you.

Check List

I t is easy to forget something when you have so many things on your mind and much to do. I find it wise to create a checklist when making my Saturday errands. Sometimes, I get distracted while grocery shopping by a sale or an intriguing meal option I may want to try. Once I get off track, it is easy to forget what I plan to pick up in that section of the store.

It would be wise in our day-to-day routines to create a checklist. It doesn't necessarily need to be on paper but mentally. It is so easy to get off course in life. We need to check ourselves in our decisions, our character, and our relationship with God. Remember to pray about every choice, remember to trust Him, and remember His Word and commandments. Check yourself in the manner you treat and speak to others. Are you bearing fruit?

When you hold yourself accountable, the enemy knows it and will place all sorts of distractions in your path to throw you off track. Incorporating the commands and Fruits of the Spirit in our daily checklist will be the guide we need to be pleasing in the eyes of God. Check your list always in all circumstances, ensuring that your behavior is purposely upright out of obedience and not for public display.

Matthew 6:1-4

"Beware of practicing your righteousness before men to be noticed by them; otherwise you have no reward with your Father who is in heaven. "So when you give to the poor, do not sound a trumpet before you, as the hypocrites do in the synagogues and in the streets, so that they may be honored by men Truly I say to you, they have their reward in full. "But when you give to the poor, do not let your left hand know what your right hand is doing, read more. so that your giving will be in secret; and your Father who sees what is done in secret will reward you.

Matthew 24:42-44

"Therefore be on the alert, for you do not know which day your Lord is coming. "But be sure of this, that if the head of the house had known at what time of the night the thief was coming, he would have been on the alert and would not have allowed his house to be broken into. "For this reason you also must be ready; for the Son of Man is coming at an hour when you do not think He will.

John 15:2

"Every branch in Me that does not bear fruit, He takes away; and every branch that bears fruit, He prunes it so that it may bear more fruit.

God's Empowering

As one develops and matures in life, the recognition of gifted abilities is noted. You realize that there are certain activities and things you like. You may favor dancing, singing, writing, creating, and maybe speaking. Some people have several abilities that may be bestowed without limitation. When you love what you are doing and do it well, you have evidence of your special ability.

Our abilities are enhanced, and growth in skills comes when we desire to research and practice what we absorb in our studies of our gifts. All abilities are a blessing from God; without Him, we could do nothing. Once we have developed a relationship with God and He reveals to us our purpose, we should ask God to guide and direct our steps. What a marvelous thing it is to know who God made you to be and that he loves you no matter what. That is spiritual empowerment of the highest order.

"God is amazing" trusting and faithfully allowing Him to pour into us what we need; He will empower our abilities according to His will for us. We will then experience and discover assurance and goodness within us that we were not aware of.

Philippians 2:13 for it is God who works in you both to will and to do for His good pleasure.

When you develop an intense desire to excel in your gift you are tapping into the greater power which is the source much bigger than you. God our creator mastered us for a special purpose and we should be grateful and thank Him continuously. He deserves all the glory.

Psalm 90:17 (KJV)

And let the beauty of the LORD our God be upon us,

And establish the work of our hands for us; Yes, establish the work of our hands.

Isaiah 64:8 (NKJV)

But now, O LORD, you are our Father; We are the clay, and You our potter; And all we are the work of Your hand.

It Didn't Work Out

Disappointed because your plan, relationship, and move didn't work out. All that we plan are not in accordance with what God has purposed in our walk of life. Often, we want something, but when it does not work out it is looked at as being negative. We almost never view denial as being positive. Trust God when He shuts a door and praise Him in the hallway until He opens another door.

Romans 8:28 (NKJV)

28 And we know that all things work together for good to those who love God, to those who are the called according to His purpose.

Many denied circumstances were blessings that prevented a bad situation or a distraction from what God has planned. Nothing or no one is greater than God and His desires for our lives.

Exodus 9:16 (NW)

16 But indeed for this purpose I have raised you up, that I may show My power in you, and that My name may be declared in all the earth.

Proverbs 15:22 (NKJV)

22 Without counsel, plans go awry, But in the multitude of counselors they are established.

Proverbs 19:21 (NKJV)

There are many plans in a man's heart; nevertheless, the Lord's counsel—that will stand.

Shut the Door

We always look forward to progression in our life circumstances. We are hopeful in our relationships, in our jobs, and in family situations. It is a natural and human desire to want the best out of what we have presently. Sometimes, our complacency can be a handicap.

Most people panic when they see and know a door is shutting. The feeling of defeat supersedes any thought of it being a blessing or new opportunity. When you trust God and give all circumstances to Him, believe His promises. He promises to never leave or forsake you. He will supply all your needs.

Many times, God has blessings for us, and we are not in a position to receive them. We have to trust His will and plan. If you reflect on something you were trying to hold on to and finally let go, only to recognize the blessing God had in store.

You realize that instead of holding on, you would have asked God to shut the door sooner. Never hold yourself hostage to people, places, or things. Always know that with God, a closed door is a new blessing or a new opportunity.

Philippians 4:19

But my God shall supply all your need according to his riches in glory by Christ Jesus.

2 Corinthians 9:8

And God is able to make all grace abound toward you; that ye, always having all sufficiency in all things, may abound to every good work

Jeremiah 17:7-8

"But blessed is the one who trusts in the Lord, whose confidence is in him. They will be like a tree planted by the water that sends out its roots by the stream. It does not fear when heat comes; its leaves are always green. It has no worries in a year of drought and never fails to bear fruit."

Spiritually Challenged

D aily, we are all challenged to make choices to either do the right thing or to do the wrong thing. Let there be no confusion when choosing to do the wrong things, speak in an ungodly manner and perform evil deeds. We are led by deception from the enemy and living in our flesh.

It is imperative that we accept Jesus Christ as our Savior, praying daily to be purged and sanctified to be led by the Holy Spirit in all that we do and all that we say. The manifestation of the Holy Spirit in us delights in the fruits of the Spirit: Love, Joy, Peace, Longsuffering, Kindness, Goodness, Faithfulness, Gentleness, and Self-control.

God has made provision for our weaknesses and knows we may fall short and commit sin. We are not held hostage by the Holy Spirit but, however must use wisdom, receive conviction, and make a choice to change and faithfully trust God's will and God's way. Living a life filled with the Holy Spirit is a desire God has for all His sheep, transforming us into the likeness and image of His Son, a Holy person.

Galatians 5:22-23 (NIV)

22 But the fruit of the Spirit is love, joy, peace, longsuffering, kindness, goodness, faithfulness,

23 gentleness, self-control. Against such there is no law.

Romans 12:2 (NKJV)

2 And do not be conformed to this world, but be transformed by the renewing of your mind, that you may prove what is that good and acceptable and perfect will of God.

Titus 3:5-7 (NIV)

5 not by works of righteousness which we have done, but according to His mercy He saved us, through the washing of regeneration and renewing of the Holy Spirit,

Silence Power

A well-known expression and truth is the statement that silence is golden. In some situations and conversations, I have learned that silence can have power. Often, we respond too rapidly and give power over another individual by revealing our insight or possible weakness.

In some situations, it may be to your advantage to maintain your composure and withhold sharing your thoughts. Your power is in being silent; the other person may not need to know how you feel now. Sometimes, it is better to listen and learn. Taking the opportunity to hear and pray about the other opinion may very well allow compromising and weighing the difference, which may lead to a greater outcome.

God has the answers we need, and when we take things to Him in prayer, the outcome may not be at all what we expect. He will work things out. Additionally, silently meditating and listening to God is a powerful way to obtain His wisdom, truth, and purpose.

John 10:27 (NKJV)

27 My sheep hear My voice, and I know them, and they follow Me.

Deuteronomy 26:17-19 (KJV)

17 Thou hast avouched the Lord this day to be thy God, and to walk in his ways, and to keep his statutes, and his commandments, and his judgments, and to hearken unto his voice:

Psalm 86:6 (KJV)

6 Give ear, O Lord, unto my prayer; and attend to the voice of my supplications.

Matthew 6:6-7 (NKJV)

But you, when you pray, go into your room, and when you have shut your door, pray to your Father who is in the secret place; and your Father who sees in secret will reward you openly.

Emptiness

Some people feel lonely because they are not involved in a relationship. Those who have lost loved ones or immediate family members often feel emptiness. Perhaps this incomplete feeling may derive from a divorce or the children growing up and moving out. People who have not accomplished what they desired in life may feel empty and unaccomplished.

A spirit of emptiness may come naturally for some. They may not feel any defining attributes, have low self-esteem and are not in a relationship with God. We are never alone, and we have fullness with the love of Jesus. One must open their heart and mind and acknowledge His presence.

The lonely must recognize that their emptiness is not due to other people, accomplishments, or status quo and that these things do not validate and fulfill. Our fulfillment is in the Lord, our joy, our peace and trust in him, so that we can overflow with hope by the power of the Holy Spirit.

Colossians 2:9-10 (NKJV)

9 For in Him dwells all the fullness of the Godhead bodily;

10 and you are complete in Him, who is the head of all principality and power.

Matthew 28:20 (NKJV)

20 teaching them to observe all things that I have commanded you; and

10, I am with you always, even to the end of the age." Amen.

Psalm 27:10 (NKJV)

When my father and my mother forsake me, then the Lord will take care of me.

Joshua 1:5 (NKJV)

5 No man shall be able to stand before you all the days of your life; as I was with Moses, so I will be with you. I will not leave you nor forsake you.

Palace or Prison

B iblically speaking, we know that our bodies are our temple that houses our spirit and soul. God created each one of us as an individual with different features, shapes, and sizes. As we mature, we recognize the things that are not healthy but may continue to indulge ourselves in an unhealthy lifestyle.

Some people are not happy with their temple and suffer from low self-esteem, envy, and jealousy of others. Is your temple a palace or a prison? How do you feel about you? I thank God for His marvelous work. Therefore, I will not be changing my nose, getting eyebrows removed then tattooed on, thinning my lips, or getting implants anywhere in my palace.

Psalm 139:13-14 (NKJV)

13 For You formed my inward parts; You covered me in my mother's womb.

14 I will praise You, for I am fearfully and wonderfully made; Marvelous are Your works, And that my soul knows very well.

How excellent are the works of our Creator? In your mind you have created a prison of dissatisfaction and therefore feel imprisoned in a castle that you should be grateful for. Confer with the Father. He can change your heart and you will appreciate the wonderful you that He created.

Genesis 1:27 (NKJV)

27 So God created man in His own image; in the image of God He created him; male and female He created them.

Jeremiah 1:5 (KJV)

5 "Before I formed you in the womb I knew you; Before you were born I sanctified you; I ordained you a prophet to the nations."

Psalm 51:10-11 (NKJV)

10 Create in me a clean heart, O God, And renew a steadfast spirit within me. 11 Do not cast me away from Your presence, And do not take Your Holy Spirit from me.

Out of the Same Mouth

You pray you praise, speak words of truth, and give honor to God. Yet out of your mouth, you curse, belittle, and slander another. Out of anger, you may feel provoked to speak in such an ungodly manner. Some people just have filthy mouths, and every other word is a curse word. There are those who think that it is just a down-to-earth way of communication and think it is cool.

I have noticed that the present-day generation thinks it is cute to speak vulgarity publicly. Perhaps they have not been taught that it is inappropriate, disrespectful and ungodly. Quite often, they do what they see their parents do. Apples don't fall far from the tree. Not only is speaking profanity a sign of ignorance it also indicates a limited vocabulary. Most important it is not pleasing to God.

Proverbs 12:18 (NKJV)

18 There is one who speaks like the piercings of a sword, But the tongue of the wise promotes health.

The words we speak should be acceptable in the sight of God. Pray for spiritual growth and ask God to rebuke the spirit of speaking filth and vulgarity.

Psalm 19:14 (NKJV)

14 Let the words of my mouth and the meditation of my heart Be acceptable in Your sight, O Lord, my strength and my Redeemer.

Ephesians 5:4 (KJV)

4 neither filthiness, nor foolish talking, nor coarse jesting, which are not fitting, but rather giving of thanks.

Romans 3:13-14 (NKJV)

13 "Their throat is an open tomb; With their tongues they have practiced deceit"; "The poison of asps is under their lips"; 14 "Whose mouth is full of cursing and bitterness."

Luke 6:45 (NKJV)

45 A good man out of the good treasure of his heart brings forth good; and an evil man out of the evil treasure of his heart brings forth evil. For out of the abundance of the heart his mouth speaks.

Your Story

As Christians, we recognize that everyone has a history and a story. Some people have more than one story. Some people are always willing to share and talk about the history of others. The unduly curious may inquire about the stories of others as well as ask questions about your history. You may recognize that they are prying and not asking out of concern.

If a person wants to give testimony or, perhaps in conversation decide to share the story of their past it should be by choice. A person should never feel obligated to reveal personal details of their life before salvation. Nor is it fair to expose their personal history without permission. What is important is that you have accepted Christ as your savior and have changed your lifestyle.

2 Corinthians 5:17 (KJV)

17 Therefore, if anyone is in Christ, he is a new creation; old things have passed away; behold, all things have become new.

Without benefit to the person exposing others' history, you wonder why someone would want to rehash the sin and unrighteousness of another. As a Christian, you are focused on where God is leading you, and they want to know where you have been. Jesus suffered to sanctify the people and by His blood we have been justified. His blood cleansed us of our sins and unrighteousness.

1John 1:9 (NKJV)

9 If we confess our sins, He is faithful and just to forgive us our sins and to cleanse us from all unrighteousness

Psalm 51:2-4 (NKJV)

2 Wash me thoroughly from my iniquity, And cleanse me from my sin.

3 For I acknowledge my transgressions, and my sin is always before me.

4 Against You, you only, have I sinned, and done this evil in Your sight— that You may be found just when You speak, and blameless when You judge.

You Never Know Who

I n life, there are all sorts of possibilities, situations, misfortunes, and the list goes on. Sometimes, you may be asked to extend yourself by helping or to assist someone else in a situation. They are not well and need help with errands or in-home assistance. Whatever their need, you must decide whether you want to or can make the sacrifice. You were quite taken with the fact that the individual came to you in the first place. The two of you have never really been close friends, and you don't communicate that often.

Additionally, over the years, you have had several disagreements. We must move past those things and consider that you never know who may need you. You may very well need someone to come to your aide one day as well. Sometimes in life, we may be called to do things that we never expected. Keep in mind that you never know who you may need or must depend on.

God may use those you least expect to come to your rescue. As Christians, we must be obedient and display brotherly kindness toward one another. God instructs us to treat others with love and kindness. We are going to be held accountable by

God for how we treat others. God wants us to deal with others, not as they treat us but as He cares for us.

Romans 15:1-7 (NKJV)

1 We then who are strong ought to bear with the scruples of the weak, and not to please ourselves.

Galatians 6:2 (NKJV)

Bear one another's burdens, and so fulfill the law of Christ.

Philippians 2:3-4 (NKJV)

Let nothing be done through selfish ambition or conceit, but in lowliness of mind let each esteem others better than himself. 4 Let each of you look out not only for his own interests, but also for the interests of others.

Early Worship

D o not rob yourself of the benefits of worship. Praising and worshipping God when you rise in the morning prompts His Holy presence. How pleasing that must be for God to see His sheep recognizing Him and His greatness and importance, acknowledging Him before anything else. Spiritually bonding with God daily brings such a pleasant and peaceful atmosphere. As you humble yourself in the greatness of His glory His peace penetrates your inner being. James 4:8 Draw near to God, and he will draw near to you. Recognize the awesome power of being in the presence of The Lord. Relief from stressful thoughts as you release all issues, obstacles, and inhibitions that the day presents. Give God complete control of everything that holds your thoughts and heart captive. During devotional time, inclusive of scriptural reading, relevant principles are derived, and personal evangelism is developed. Practice and dedication of this personal time with God daily also develop a closer relationship. In this delegated time, the Holy Spirit manifests the intimacy and awesomeness of God as you praise and worship Him.

When you enter a life of praise and worship during the good times and in times of crisis, you will find strength and power in Him. Get into the presence of God through praise and worship, and let His hand come mightily upon you.

Psalms 8:1

0 LORD, our Lord, how majestic is your name in all the earth. You have set your glory above the heavens.

Psalms 29:2

Ascribe to the LORD the glory due his name; worship the LORD in the splendor of holiness.

Psalms 95:6

Oh come, let us worship and bow down; let us kneel before the LORD, our Maker!

Psalms 99:5

Exalt the LORD our God; worship at his footstool! Holy is he

Beneficial Deposits

I enjoy reading and quite often run into people who like to read as well. The first book I pick up daily is the Holy Bible. I utilize God's Word during my morning devotional time. This is the first installation of knowledge I pursue on a daily basis. Lots of people start their day by reading the local newspaper. Reading the newspaper is secondary during my day. Most times, I pick up the newspaper to read the long version or continuation of something that I saw on the news.

There was a time in my life when I used public transportation to commute back and forth to my workplace. I recall observing what books others were reading. During those times, black fiction was beginning to be popular. There were also those who read books pertaining to school/classes, literature pertaining to their employment or just various advertisements. My assumption is that everyday people read everyday things. I wonder how many people read the Word of God during the week. One must ask oneself are the things that you are reading are beneficial deposits.

Although we must educate ourselves in order to prosper in our careers, we must fuel our spirit and acquire wisdom that God has provided in the Book of Life, the Holy Bible. God's Word provides us with the wisdom and direction pertaining to the ways in which God wants us to live.

Acts 17:11 (KJV)

These were more noble than those in Thessalonica, in that they received the word with all readiness of mind, and searched the scriptures daily, whether those things were so.

If people today had such a desire to chase after the Word of God as they do fictional stories. By consuming the written Word of God in the Holy Bible the resource guide for life, we are acquiring beneficial deposits daily. I have read a tremendous number of books covering several areas of life. I personally find the Word of God to be the one book that covers any and every area I need to experience growth.

Proverbs 1:7 (NKJV)

The fear of the LORD is the beginning of knowledge, But fools despise wisdom and instruction.

Proverbs 4:5-7

Get wisdom, get understanding: forget it not; neither decline from the words of my mouth. Forsake her not, and she shall preserve thee: love her, and she shall keep thee. Wisdom is the principal thing; therefore, get wisdom: and with all thy getting get understanding.

Proverbs 10:13

In the lips of him that hath understanding wisdom is found: but a rod is for the back of him that is void of understanding.

Mindful of How You

Treat Others

I n a Christian environment, it is deplorable when people are treated unkindly, unfairly or dismissed as unimportant. Many in leadership and management positions favor those of popular status and public icons. All of God's children are purposeful and important.

Too often, growth and public recognition can fascinate, distract, and give a person the idea of dominance and superiority. Unfortunately, this falsehood is prevailing in the Christian environment. Such obsession with status pro causes the Christian to strive to impress others versus extending credence in what is truth.

The impossible and improbable occurrences that surface in the Christian life are blessings and confirmation of what God is capable of. Our confidence and trust in God can and will be challenged in many ways. The enemy will attack your blessings and fulfilled desires, causing you to misuse what God has made possible.

Excessive pride causes arrogance, pride fullness and boasting of achievements and possessions. This ostentatious behavior, show of importance and wealth, looking down on others, and treating people as if they are unworthy is a spirit that God is not pleased with. Be mindful of how you treat others. God uses the least of the and can elevate as well as humble those full of pride.

Jeremiah 9:23 (NKJV)

23 Thus says the Lord: "Let not the wise man glory in his wisdom, Let not the mighty man glory in his might, Nor let the rich man glory in his riches;

Isaiah 23:9 (NW)

9 The Lord of hosts has purposed it, To bring to dishonor the pride of all glory, To bring into contempt all the honorable of the earth.

Phillipians 2:3 (ESV)

Do nothing from selfish ambition or conceit, but in humility count others more significant than yourselves.

Great Performers

A multitude of people are bestowed with the ability to act and perform. In the arts of theatrics and music, there are extended amounts of opportunities to exhibit one's great talents. These gifted talents can be used in the wrong way as well.

In the Church, talented people can sing but may not have an anointing. Their voice can still minister music to the Congregation. Just like the talent to sing, there are people that have the gift to gab. A preacher may know the scriptures and deliver an excellent message. Some people have learned to act like a Christian. God is not looking for actors!!!!

A true believer of God (a Christian), changes start in their heart. Their behavior and spoken words reveal the heart. A Christian loves Christ and keeps His commands. A Christian serves the one and only true living God. The actions of a Christian are not judgmental or hypocritical.

God is not in need of great performers. He desires Kingdom-minded disciples and humble servants seeking to worship and live throughout eternity in His Glory.

Matthew 15:8 (NKJV)

8 'These people draw near to Me with their mouth, And honor Me with their lips, But their heart is far from Me.

James 1:26 (NKJV)

26 If anyone among you[a] thinks he is religious, and does not bridle his tongue but deceives his own heart, this one's religion is useless.

Isaiah 29:13 (NKJV)

13 Therefore the Lord said "Inasmuch as these people draw near with their mouths And honor Me with their lips, But have removed their hearts far from Me, And their fear toward Me is taught by the commandment of men,

1 John 2:9 (NKJV)

9 He who says he is in the light, and hates his brother, is in darkness until now.

God Gave It to You

Our personal desires are just that; whether we pursue them is up to us. Sometimes, what we desire is not what God has purposed for our lives. Individually, God bestows us. Some people have multiple gifts—all according to His will.

Too often, we use our gifts for the wrong purpose. That is not to say God is displeased if we are not misusing our gifts for evil. Our purpose and season will prevail in God's timing. We may also lose focus on our own gifts, envying and desiring to operate another's gift.

What God has for you is for you. Although you are bestowed in many ways, your modus operandi may not be what God has purposed. Wanting what others have can throw you off track. If you don't know your purpose, seek God, and He will direct your path. When God reveals to you where you will thrive, be grateful and allow Him to develop what He has entrusted to you.

Prayer and relationship with God is key in His revealing of wisdom and understanding of how to operate in your gift. God gave you specific characteristics to fulfill your call and He will establish His will.

James 1:17 (KJV)

17 "Every good gift and every perfect gift is from above, and cometh down from the Father of lights, with whom is no variableness, neither shadow of turning."

Romans 12:6 (KJV)

6 Having then gifts differing according to the grace that is given to us, whether prophecy, let us prophesy according to the proportion of faith;

1 Corinthians 12:1-8(KJV)

1 Now concerning spiritual gifts, brethren, I would not have you ignorant.

2 Ye know that ye were Gentiles, carried away unto these dumb idols, even as ye were led.

3 Wherefore I give you to understand, that no man speaking by the Spirit of God calleth Jesus accursed: and that no man can say that Jesus is the Lord, but by the Holy Ghost.

4 Now there are diversities of gifts, but the same Spirit.

5 And there are differences of administrations, but the same Lord.

6 And there are diversities of operations, but it is the same God which worketh all in all.

7 But the manifestation of the Spirit is given to every man to profit withal.

8 For to one is given by the Spirit the word of wisdom; to another the word of knowledge by the same Spirit;

Great Reflection

T raditionally during the time of year spent with family sharing the festivities of the Christmas Holiday. Many focus on gifts to purchase for a loved one as well as the gifts we may want to receive. Special attention is given to decorating indoors as well as out. So much of our time is spent doing, going, and spending.

If we were to use our imagination and think about the rejoicing and celebration going on in Heaven when the Son of God was earthly born, representing the greatest gift to mankind. All focus surrounded the King of Kings and Lord of Lords. A Master Plan was now in effect, and it cost us nothing.

There is sufficient reason to celebrate. However, could we give up the costly traditions and misperceptions of the season and focus on God and His unselfish presence. Christmas time is a great time to reflect on the Deity and blessing of His eternal gift. A gift that keeps on giving.

1 John 5:11 (NKJV)

And this is the testimony: God has given us eternal life, and this life is in his Son.

Romans 6:23 (NW)

For the wages of sin is death, but the gift of God is eternal life in Christ Jesus our Lord.

John 3:16 (NKJV)

For God so loved the world that he gave his one and only Son, that whoever believes in him shall not perish but have eternal life.

Titus 3:4-7 (NIV)

But when the kindness and the love of God our Savior toward man appeared, not by works of righteousness which we have done, but according to His mercy He saved us, through the washing of regeneration and renewing of the Holy Spirit, whom He poured out on us abundantly through Jesus Christ our Savior, that having been justified by His grace we should become heirs according to the hope of eternal life.

The Closer You Get

I t is exciting when you are traveling to a new or different destination when you see or are informed that you are almost there. Many plans may allow you to experience new adventures, sights, foods, and people; the anticipation and enthusiasm heighten the closer you get to new pleasures.

Keep in mind the greatness of God's peace and fulfilling joy. The closer we get to His purpose in our lives, the greater the challenges and warfare. These distractions can be in many forms of attack. Therefore, we should be mindful to exercise more prayer, trust, and faith in God. Allow Him to direct your path.

God is fully aware of every challenge and all our trials. He is in complete control. No enemy attack is greater than His Power. Just as we anticipate new experiences and adventures, we plan, trust and believe that God has a great plan predestined for your life. Whatever the journey, no matter how rough the road may be, know that the closer you are to what God has for you.

Jeremiah 29:11 (KJV)

11 For I know the thoughts that I think toward you, saith the LORD, thoughts of peace, and not of evil, to give you an expected end.

Ephesians 2:10 (KJV)

10 For we are his workmanship, created in Christ Jesus unto good works, which God Kath before ordained that we should walk in them.

Psalms 138:8 (KJV)

8 The LORD will perfect that which concerneth me: thy mercy, O LORD, endureth for ever: forsake not the works of thine own hands.

Jeremiah 1:5 (KJV)

5 Before I formed thee in the belly I knew thee; and before thou camest forth out of the womb I sanctified thee, [and] I ordained thee a prophet unto the nations.

Plan It

Daily, we make all sorts of plans. We plan our day, we plan for the week, and much focus is on weekend plans. Vacations are planned and maybe scheduled for the next year.

Many have vices or negative character traits that are frequently indulged in. How many times have you mentioned that you were going to stop doing this or stop doing that? Plan to stop or quit these ungodly indulgences and behavior.

If only we would put forth the same determination and effort to do the things pleasing to God as we do those pleasures we desire. Positive change is hopeful and supported by meaningful relations. More importantly, God affirms us when living a righteous and wholesome life.

God's affirmation of our lives manifests gifts and purpose. Our Spiritual gifts enable us to function in a pleasurable way in the eyes of God through unique contributions to others. He will give us wisdom to operate and develop in His Master Plan. The greatest and most significant plan ever made.

Matthew 6:25-34 (ESV)

"Therefore, I tell you, do not be anxious about your life, what you will eat or what you will drink, nor about your body, what you will put on. Is not life more than food, and the body more than clothing? Look at the birds of the air: they neither sow nor reap nor gather into barns, and yet your heavenly Father feeds them. Are you not of more value than they? And which of you by being anxious can add a single hour to his span of life? And why are you anxious about clothing? Consider the lilies of the field, how they grow: they neither toil nor spin, yet I tell you, even Solomon in all his glory was not arrayed like one of these. ...

Jeremiah 29:11-14 (ESV)

For I know the plans I have for you, declares the Lord, plans for welfare and not for evil, to give you a future and a hope. Then you will call upon me and come and pray to me, and I will hear you. You will seek me and find me, when you seek me with all your heart. I will be found by you, declares the Lord, and I will restore your fortunes and gather you from all the nations and all the places where I have driven you, declares the Lord, and I will bring you back to the place from which I sent you into exile.

Hebrews 12:5-11 (ESV)

And have you forgotten the exhortation that addresses you as sons? "My son, do not regard lightly the discipline of the Lord, nor be weary when reproved by him. For the Lord disciplines the one he loves, and chastises every son whom he receives." It is for discipline that you have to endure. God is treating you as sons. For what son is there whom his father does not discipline? If you are left without discipline, in which all have participated, then you are illegitimate children and not sons. Besides this, we have had earthly fathers who disciplined us and we respected them. Shall we not much more be subject to the Father of spirits and live?

Preparation

Some of us may start to prepare for events, birthdays, and holidays in advance. We intend to have things work out per the desired way we celebrate the occasion. We make purchases, read up on new recipes and may make changes in our home or locate a venue.

We always make plans to do and celebrate occasions and milestones in our lives. However, the most important focus in our preparation should be incorporating God and His directives into our lives. Our preparation to be and do what God has purposed for us should be our main goal. To no avail, the enemy will do all and anything using anybody he can to distract us.

In our prep, we must put on the full armor and equip ourselves for warfare. The devil knows where we are destined to go and be, and his constant plan is to plot, placing obstacles and distractions.

Live and exemplify the Fruits of the Spirit. Reach for your destiny, and strive to be the best of you in God by righteousness, love, and peace. There will be a celebration beyond measures at the end of this life in Glory with the Father, Son, and Holy Spirit as we enter His presence. No greater event to prepare for.

Ephesians 6:10-12 (NKJV)

10 Finally, my brethren, be strong in the Lord and in the power of His might.

11 Put on the whole armor of God, that you may be able to stand against the wiles of the devil.

12 For we do not wrestle against flesh and blood, but against principalities, against powers, against the rulers of the darkness of this age, against spiritual hosts of wickedness in the heavenly places.

Galatians 5:22-23 (NKJV)

22 But the fruit of the Spirit is love, joy, peace, longsuffering, kindness, goodness, faithfulness,

23 gentleness, self-control. Against such there is no law.

Ephesians 1:3-14 (NKJV)

Blessed be the God and Father of our Lord Jesus Christ, who has blessed us with every spiritual blessing in the heavenly places in Christ, just as He chose us in Him before the foundation of the world, that we would be holy and blameless before Him In love He predestined us to adoption as sons through Jesus Christ to Himself, according to the kind intention of His will, to the praise of the glory of His grace, which He freely bestowed on us in the Beloved. In Him we have redemption through His blood, the forgiveness of our trespasses, according to the riches of His grace which He lavished on us. In all wisdom and insight, He made known to us the mystery of His will, according to His kind intention which He purposed in Him with a view to an administration suitable to the fullness of the times, that is, the summing up of all things in Christ, things in the heavens and things on the earth. In Him also we have obtained an inheritance, having been predestined according to His purpose who works all things after the counsel of His will, to the end that we Who were the first to hope in Christ would be to the praise of His glory. In Him, you also, after listening to the message of truth, the gospel of your salvation--having also believed, you were sealed in Him with the Holy Spirit of promise, who is given as a pledge of our inheritance, with a view to the redemption of God's own possession, to the praise of His glory.

Stand Strong

I n our lives, we may face many obstacles and circumstances. Quite often, we find ourselves in a position where we need to make decisions. On an average, it is just a matter of making a choice. Faith should cancel our worries if we keep God in the loop and always make choices according to His directives.

Sometimes, everything seems to fall apart, and your world feels upside down. We complain, we worry, and we place blame. These feelings of defeat affect our attitude and how we treat others. If you trust God, then trust Him always in every situation. At the end of the day, all things are in His control. Nothing gets past His infinite knowledge.

Take a stand in His Word, take a stand in what you believe, take a stand in your faith, and let it not waiver. Let your stance and attitude be positive in an upright position. Stand strong in God and watch Him work all things together for the good of Him.

Ephesians 3:16-17 (NKJV)

16 that He would grant you, according to the riches of His glory, to be strengthened with might through His Spirit in the inner man,

17 that Christ may dwell in your hearts through faith; that you, being rooted and grounded in love,

Romans 15:13 (NKJV)

13 Now may the God of hope fill you with all joy and peace in believing, that you may abound in hope by the power of the Holy Spirit.

Hebrews 11:1-6 (NKJV)

1 Now faith is the substance of things hoped for, the evidence of things not seen.

2 For by it the elders obtained a good testimony.

3 By faith we understand that the worlds were framed by the word of God, so that the things which are seen were not made of things which are visible.

4 By faith Abel offered to God a more excellent sacrifice than Cain, through which he obtained witness that he was righteous, God testifying of his gifts; and through it he being dead still speaks.

5 By faith Enoch was taken away so that he did not see death, "and was not found, because God had taken him"; for before he was taken he had this testimony, that he pleased God.

6 But without faith it is impossible to please Him, for he who comes to God must believe that He is, and that He is a rewarder of those who diligently seek Him.

What About Tomorrow?

We have no idea from day to day what tomorrow holds. We make plans and have expectations that may or may not unfold. The essential point is we can only rely on what God has purposed and allotted for us. Our measure of faith and obedience is key in our portion daily.

Mathew 6:34

Take therefore no thought for the morrow: for the morrow shall take thought for the things of itself. Sufficient unto the day is the evil thereof. A scripture that has meaning equated to the sufficiency of one's faith in God day by day, not worrying or being anxious for nothing. Each day has its own challenges and troubles.

Yet still, tomorrow cannot be taken for granted. Tomorrow is not promised. We should live in accordance with God's commands and guidance.

Clearly reminds us that life is like a vapor and can vanish at any time. Walking in relationship with God living according to His will excepting Jesus Christ as your Savior benefits us the promise of eternal life with the Father. Is your tomorrow an eternal promise?

James 4:14 (NKJV)

14 whereas you do not know what will happen tomorrow. For what is your life? It is even a vapor that appears for a little time and then vanishes away.

John 3:36 (NKJV)

36 He who believes in the Son has everlasting life; and he who does not believe the Son shall not see life, but the wrath of God abides on him."

Galatians 6:9 (NIV)

9 And let us not grow weary while doing good, for in due season we shall reap if we do not lose heart.

Earthly Good

We live day to day, focusing on our jobs, our possessions, and the family and people we relate to. These are very important factors, however, where the unbalance lies are usually vices and entertainment. So many people realize later in life that they have wasted precious time fulfilling worldly purposes versus being kingdom-minded.

It is easily overlooked and not recognized God's earthly purposes for us. Our relationship with God is key to finding our purpose. Earthly good and purpose are crucial to us in our desire and quest for eternal life. Although some distractions are lessons for reproof and wisdom, it is our responsibility to distinguish between our personal desires and God's will for us.

Let your focus surround the spiritual fruits versus those temporal things. Honestly measure your earthly good to see if it is deserving of His eternal promises. God promises and Biblical guidance is sure proof. God is a God of truth, and if He said it.... faithfully trust Him. Allow Him to be your portion of earthly good to be Heavenly bound!!!

Deuteronomy 7:9 NKJV

Know therefore that the LORD your God, he is God, the faithful God, who keeps covenant and mercy with them that love him and keep his commandments to a thousand generations;

Joshua 23:14 NASB

Now behold, today I am going the way of all the earth, and you know in all your hearts and in all your souls that not one word of all the good words which the LORD your God spoke concerning you has failed; all have been fulfilled for you, not one of them has failed.

2 Peter 1:4 KJV

Whereby are given unto us exceeding great and precious promises: that by these ye might be partakers of the divine nature, having escaped the corruption that is in the world through lust.

At The End Of The Day

M ost of us has a bit of structure and a planned schedule for our day. Too often, our days become routine. We arise, and some may pray and devote time to God, eat breakfast and prepare to go to work. We work an average of eight hours a day. Once we are back home, we complete our evening with dinner, domestic tasks, maybe watch a little television then prepare for bed.

Our days are, for the most part, repetitious. At the end of the day, have you pleased God? Have you followed His purposed plan? Do you know your purpose? Unfortunately, many people have no idea of their worth. If you don't know your worth, you may feel unworthy to fill the gifts and purposed plan God has designed for you. Understanding that God's infinite wisdom knows the best path for our lives.

God created everyone with a purpose. We were called to worship and glorify Him. To understand, you must first believe and be born again in Christ. The Holy Spirit then leads and guides you per the will of God. Freely submit to the commands, and the Word of God is full proof of His promise. So, ask yourself, at the end of the day, have I done all I can do on this day to please God?

Exodus 9:16 (NW)

But indeed, for this purpose, I have raised you up, that I may show My power in you, and that My name may be declared in all the earth.

Romans 12:2 (NKJV)

And do not be conformed to this world, but be transformed by the renewing of your mind, that you may prove what is that good and acceptable and perfect will of God.

Jeremiah 29: 11 (AMP)

For I know the thoughts and plans that I have for you, says the Lord, thoughts and plans for welfare and peace and not for evil, to give you hope in your final outcome.

2 Timothy 1:9 (NKJV)

Who has saved us and called us with a holy calling, not according to our works, but according to His own purpose and grace which was given to us in Christ Jesus before time began.

Right There

C hildren learn at an early age to be sneaky and deceitful. I guess it is a behavior that comes naturally until it is corrected. Oftentimes, they pick up things and put them in their mouths, and when caught, they try to avoid you removing the object. A toddler learns to run away when the question is what you have in your hand, knowing it is something they were told not to touch.

Some adults maintain this deceitful and sneaky behavior. They do things in private in hopes of not being discovered. People will exhaust all means to cover up their sinful ways. Apparently, they never stop and consider that others may not know your secrets, but God is right there. He sees all, hears all, and knows all. God can reveal your secrets if it is in His will to do so.

Never think for one moment that you can deceive God. God never sleeps nor slumbers, and at the end of the day, we should be more concerned about how He sees us. Negative character and unrighteous behavior are displeasing to Him. He gives us opportunities to repent, be saved, and forgiven. Many still may not change their harmful behavior. How do we not respect the fact that He is right there during it all?

We must stay focused and recognize and respect His omnipotent presence. It is so easy to fall back into living your life at your free will without considering the condemnation that lies ahead. Disobedience and unrighteousness have consequences. Always trust and know that God is right there.

Hebrews 4:13 (NW)

13 And there is no creature hidden from His sight, but all things are naked and open to the eyes of Him to whom we must give account.

Psalm 139:1-6 (NKJV)

1 O Lord, you have searched me and known me. 2 You know my sitting down and my rising up; You understand my thought afar off. 3 You comprehend my path and my lying down, And are acquainted with all my ways. 4 For there is not a word on my tongue, But behold, O Lord, you know it altogether. 5 You have hedged me behind and before, And laid Your hand upon me. 6 Such knowledge is too wonderful for me; It is high, I cannot attain it.

Galatians 6:7-10 (NKJV)

7 Do not be deceived, God is not mocked; for whatever a man sows, that he will also reap. 8 For he who sows to his flesh will of the flesh reap corruption, but he who sows to the Spirit will of the Spirit reap everlasting life. 9 And let us not grow weary while doing good, for in due season we shall reap if we do not lose heart. 10 Therefore, as we have opportunity, let us do good to all, especially to those who are of the household of faith.

Thought Aloud

Sometimes, our thoughts tickle us, and we may laugh aloud. Others around you ask you what is so funny? You may share, or it may very well be something that you don't wish to share. The mind is an inner, subjective state of consciousness. It is estimated that a human brain produces as many as 12,000 to 50,000 thoughts per day, depending on how deep a thinker a person is.

Imagine all your thoughts being heard by others. Would your thoughts be righteous and Godly? Many of our thoughts could embarrass others, be hurtful and displeasing. Our thoughts can be our worst enemy.

Allowing the enemy to plant unhealthy seeds can be fatal. It is our responsibility to eliminate and control our thoughts. Is God pleased with your thoughts?

An active prayer life and relationship with God helps our focus and thinking. Keeping God active in our lives allowing Him to order our steps and lead our path is key. He knows our weaknesses and the plots and plans of the enemy. God is our Keeper, He keeps our thoughts, our hearts and our strength. When we trust Him, He empowers us to conquer our weak areas.

Be mindful of God. He never leaves or forsakes you. Free your mind of evil and sinful thoughts and temptations. Focus on His ways and what is pleasing in His sight. Guard your heart and guard your mind.

Romans 12:2 (NW)

2 And do not be conformed to this world, but be transformed by the renewing of your mind, that you may prove what is that good and acceptable and perfect will of God.

Philippians 4:8 (NKJV)

8 Finally, brethren, whatever things are true, whatever things are noble, whatever things are just, whatever things are pure, whatever things are lovely, whatever things are of good report, if there is any virtue and if there is anything praiseworthy—meditate on these things.

Ephesians 4:22-32 (NKJV)

22 that you put off, concerning your former conduct, the old man which grows corrupt according to the deceitful lusts,

23 and be renewed in the spirit of your mind,

24 and that you put on the new man which was created according to God, in true righteousness and holiness.

25 Therefore, putting away lying, "Let each one of you speak truth with his neighbor," for we are members of one another.

26 "Be angry, and do not sin": do not let the sun go down on your wrath,

27 nor give place to the devil.

28 Let him who stole steal no longer, but rather let him labor, working with his hands what is good, that he may have something to give him who has need.

29 Let no corrupt word proceed out of your mouth, but what is good for necessary edification, that it may impart grace to the hearers.

30 And do not grieve the Holy Spirit of God, by whom you were sealed for the day of redemption.

31 Let all bitterness, wrath, anger, clamor, and evil speaking be put away from you, with all malice.

32 And be kind to one another, tenderhearted, forgiving one another, even as God in Christ forgave you.

Entitled

M any young people have a spirit of entitlement. They truly believe that the world owes them. They do things and behave outside of the realms of the law. Many are disrespectful and are not mindful of elders or their wisdom. The world does not owe you a thing.

A generation of people which have been given so much in materialistic possessions. Bestowed by parents, most of which are career-driven. This means of compensation has replaced quality family time, relationships, and responsibility.

When it comes to entitlement, we are all entitled to the benefits of salvation. We have the right and permission to pursue the love of God. We are eligible by our righteousness and obedience to His eternal promise. Jesus paid the cost in advance.

If only people would adopt that same entitled spirit to the rights Jesus has sponsored for their lives. Take advantage of your birth rights He provided in advance. There is no greater love than that of which Jesus has given. He sacrificed His life for you, and you are entitled to the benefits.

Ephesians 4:7 (NKJV)

7 But to each one of us grace was given according to the measure of Christ's gift.

2 Corinthians 9:15 (NIV)

Thanks be to God for His indescribable gift!

John 3:16 (NKJV)

16 For God so loved the world that He gave His only begotten Son, that whoever believes in Him should not perish but have everlasting life.

When You Are Perfect

W here do you start when concluding decisions on a person's character? Normally or sensibly, we consider their behavior and actions per what is right and what is wrong. In doing so, do we ever stop to think as to why a person does what they do? Do they have a negative history or upbringing? Did something happen to them to cause their acting out? Are they mentally stable?

Although, in society, persons in authority can make decisions on your behalf per your ability to respect and obey laws. God knows each one of us, and He knows our character flaws, mental inadequacies, and communal sufferings. For this very same reason, He is the only one who has the right to judge and make the final decision.

In our day-to-day relations and interactions with others, we take it upon ourselves to judge people by what we think or feel. When you are perfect and righteous, maybe God will place an assignment with you. Until then, always remember that judgement belongs to God. The Perfect Wise and True God.

Psalms 75:6-7

For not from the east or from the west and not from the wilderness comes lifting, but it is God who executes judgment, putting down one and lifting another.

Ecclesiastes 12:14

For God will bring every deed into judgment, with every secret thing, whether good or evil.

Matthew 7:2-4

For with the judgment you pronounce you will be judged, and with the measure you use it will be measured to you. Why do you see the speck that is in your brother's eye, but do not notice the log that is in your own eye? Or how can you say to your brother, 'Let me take the speck out of your eye,' when there is the log in your own eye?

Respect Your Calling

A t an early age, we are taught to respond respectfully to our parents. We may answer the call of our friends or siblings in an uncivil or insulting manner. Most children knew that they would face consequences if they answered the call of their parents or other adults in a disrespectful way.

Being called by God means laying down your life and taking heed to His purpose. Many times, God's call may challenge us because with the call comes struggles and warfare. That's right, the devil knows your calling as well and he will try in any way possible to cause you to be disobedient.

One must also accept that being called by God does not mean you will be rich or famous. The Master of the universe calls you to serve. If God calls you to a specific deed or position, it is our duty to respond respectfully and serve. Be a humble servant and acknowledge God's calling in your life.

Trust God and know that if He called you to it, He will bring you through any adversity and struggle you face. He is in total and complete control. Respect your calling!!!

John 15:16 (NIV)

16 You did not choose Me, but I chose you and appointed you that you should go and bear fruit, and that your fruit should remain, that whatever you ask the Father in My name He may give you.

2Timothy 2:9 (NKJV)

9 who has saved us and called us with a holy calling, not according to our works, but according to His own purpose and grace which was given to us in Christ Jesus before time began,

Romans 8:28 (NKJV)

28 And we know that all things work together for good to those who love God, to those who are the called according to His purpose.

Turn The Page

R eading is fundamental, but all reading is not good reading. The setting and character script can run on and may also be boring. While reading, you may decide to turn the page or maybe a few to get to the plot.

Our lives tell a story. Many times, there are circumstances and parts of it we'd like to turn the page and quickly move on past our current trials. We must stop and remember who the author is and understand that every part of the story is important for God's refining of our character.

When you desire to turn the page, be certain you are doing so to forgive, to grow, and to move past hindrances or obstacles that God has given way for deliverance. In all things, we must trust where He is leading our paths. Just know that He is the Author of the Greatest Story ever told, and your story was designed by the Great I Am.

Isaiah 43:18-19 (NKJV)

18 Do not remember the former things, Nor consider the things of old.

19 Behold, I will do a new thing, Now it shall spring forth; Shall you not know it? I will even make a road in the wilderness And rivers in the desert.

Peter 2:1-2 (NKJV)

Therefore, laying aside all malice, all deceit, hypocrisy, envy, and all evil speaking,

2 as newborn babes, desire the pure milk of the word, that you may grow thereby,

Hebrews 12:1 (NKJV)

1 Therefore we also, since we are surrounded by so great a cloud of witnesses, let us lay aside every weight, and the sin which so easily ensnares us, and let us run with endurance the race that is set before us,

Undeniable Trust

I t can be very awkward when a person inquires and asks if you trust them. I do believe that there are many levels of trust. In relationships, we trust a person for who they are and who they have proven to be. It would be fair to say that trust is circumstantial.

We feel betrayed if someone breaks our trust. Even when we forgive them, they will never regain that trust level. There is an old saying that you deal with them with a long-handle spoon. Depending on the level of hurt caused by the broken trust, you may never trust them again.

God's Word offers many scriptures on trusting Him and not humankind.

Psalms 118:8 (KJV)

[It is] better to trust in the LORD than to put confidence in man. His Word quite often reminds us to trust Him in all things. Trusting God will transform your life.

God is the Master of all creations and He is the genius of all things. He has complete control. Why trust anyone or thing but God? Trust Him in adversity, in our relationships, in our decision-making. Trust Him in all aspects of your life allowing

Him to direct your path. Our trust should be undeniable and not waver.

Proverbs 3:5 (KJV)

Trust in the LORD with all thine heart; and lean not unto thine own understanding.

Psalms 9:10 (KJV)

And they that know thy name will put their trust in thee: for thou, LORD, hast not forsaken them that seek thee.

Psalms 28:7 (KJV)

The LORD [is] my strength and my shield; my heart trusted in him, and I am helped: therefore my heart greatly rejoiceth; and with my song will I praise him.

Bitterness

It is disappointing when you take a bite from a fruit with the expectation of a sweet and pleasing taste, and it is bitter. You may very well encounter a person who is continuously angry and bitter. Their behavior is ungodly, disappointing, and unpleasant.

Acts 8:23 (NKJV)

23 For I see that you are poisoned by bitterness and bound by iniquity?

This behavior is displeasing to God as well. This crushing mental state is the result of anger, the guilt of sin, and hostility which trigger additional sins such as hatred, self-pity, vengeance, and arrogance and downright nastiness.

Romans 3:14 (NKJV)

14 "Whose mouth is full of cursing and bitterness." All of which hinders the fellowship and relationship with God.

Bitter people are antisocial, selfish, and withdrawn, and there is no ration. Most people avoid contact because there is no happiness around them. The fragmented state of a bitter person can only be changed by God. We can pray for their redemption from the bondage they are consumed and captured in.

Ephesians 4:31-32 (NKJV)

31 Let all bitterness, wrath, anger, clamor, and evil speaking be put away from you, with all malice.

32 And be kind to one another, tenderhearted, forgiving one another, even as God in Christ forgave you.

2 Corinthians 5:17 (NKJV)

17 Therefore, if anyone is in Christ, he is a new creation; old things have passed away; behold, all things have become new.

Acts 3:19 (NKJV)

19 Repent therefore and be converted, that your sins may be blotted out, so that times of refreshing may come from the presence of the Lord.

Not Here

Most of us lose sight of small possessions placed aside. Sometimes, we think about something and wonder what happened to it. You may recall placing it in a certain place only to find after searching it is not there. You are then baffled without a clue as to where it is.

In many circumstances in life, we look for something in the wrong place only to find it is not there at all. We look for love, we look for happiness, and we look for peace in people, places, and things. Yet, we find that what we want and need is not there.

Once we realize that the completeness of these things is not carnal or materialistic, we then know where to find what is not here. Peace and happiness are found within ourselves and are an outpouring of love and joy from God. He can give you peace during times of lack or trial that is unexplainable.

Nothing or no one can complete us but God. Completion and total satisfaction can only be Heavenly, and it is not here. Look to Him, who holds your future and trust His Word obediently following the commands. Your peace and completeness are promised and paid for by His Son, Jesus Christ and through Him, we find salvation and eternal life in Heaven.

John 16:33 (KJV)

33 These things I have spoken unto you, that in me ye might have peace. In the world ye shall have tribulation: but be of good cheer; I have overcome the world.

Romans 15:13 (KJV)

Now the God of hope fills you with all joy and peace in believing, that ye may abound in hope, through the power of the Holy Ghost.

1 John 5:11-13 (NKJV)

11 And this is the testimony: that God has given us eternal life, and this life is in His Son.

12 He who has the Son has life; he who does not have the Son of God does not have life.

13 These things I have written to you who believe in the name of the Son of God, that you may know that you have eternal life, and that you may continue to believe in the name of the Son of God.

Careless Love

T o maintain a healthy relationship, one must acknowledge and be attentive and respectful to others. Many relationships are broken because one partner is thoughtful, mindful, and offering quality time, and the other does not. A healthy relationship cannot be one-sided and should benefit both partners.

A lot of relationships fall through the cracks because of selfishness, dishonesty, and uncommitted participants. In many cases, one is committed, and the other is not and only communicates when they want or need something from the other. Isn't that how many people relate to God? We claim to be in a relationship with Him but only call on Him when we are in a crisis or have a need.

Too often we are careless with our love and relationship with God. Although we are careless, selfish, and not always as attentive as we should be. He is always giving, blessing, and loving us unconditionally. I am elated that God is a kind, forgiving God. If He treated us the way we carelessly treat our relationship with Him, surely it would be an awakening.

Imagine the peace and joy you would share in a committed relationship with God. Yes, there will be trials and circumstances still, but that is when your faith and trust in Him should prevail more. God is and always will be the loving, caring, forgiving being that He is.

Carefully be mindful of your relationship with Him. He is the great I Am, and through His Son, Jesus, He has given you the most important gift you will ever receive.

Romans 8:37-39 (NKJV)

37 Yet in all these things we are more than conquerors through Him who loved us.

38 For I am persuaded that neither death nor life, nor angels nor principalities nor powers, nor things present nor things to come,

39 nor height nor depth, nor any other created thing, shall be able to separate us from the love of God which is in Christ Jesus our Lord.

1 John 4:9-11 (NKJV)

9 In this the love of God was manifested toward us, that God has sent His only begotten Son into the world, that we might live through Him.

10 In this is love, not that we loved God, but that He loved us and sent His Son to be the propitiation for our sins.

11 Beloved, if God so loved us, we also ought to love one another.

1 John 4:9-11 (NKJV)

9 In this the love of God was manifested toward us, that God has sent His only begotten Son into the world, that we might live through Him.

10 In this is love, not that we loved God, but that He loved us and sent His Son to be the propitiation for our sins.

11 Beloved, if God so loved us, we also ought to love one another.

Finding Peace

M any times, we are challenged with situations that can affect the way we feel. Negative vibes and situations can take a toll on your stress level and performance. It is human nature to exercise self-defense. The important thing is how you defend the situation. It is not always what you say; it is how you say it.

There may be some people who thrive in turmoil and confusion, but I believe, for the most part, people prefer peace and serenity. A fire will eventually burn out unless you continue to fuel it. We can always find peace in troubled circumstances. When we place our trust in God and give our all to Him, He will give us peace.

God is a God of peace! His Spirit transcends all circumstances and passes our understanding. We can find inner peace when we have found peace with Him. The Fruits of His Spirit are all positive and desirable. "Tribulations" bring thoughts of trouble, anxiety, fear, and doubt. However, Paul writes in Romans 5:3-5 that those who have peace with God and access to Him glory in tribulations, knowing that tribulation produces perseverance; and perseverance, character; and character, hope. Now hope does not disappoint, because the love of God has been poured out into our hearts by the Holy Spirit which was given to us.

No matter what the circumstance is, with God, you can find peace!

2 Thessalonians 3:16

Now the Lord of peace himself give you peace always by all means. The Lord be with you all.

John 16:33

These things I have spoken unto you, that in me ye might have peace. In the world ye shall have tribulation: but be of good cheer; I have overcome the world.

Philippians 4:6

Be careful for nothing; but in everything by prayer and supplication with thanksgiving let your requests be made known unto God.

Isaiah 26:3

Thou wilt keep him in perfect peace, whose mind is stayed on thee: because he trusteth in thee

The Pandemic 2020

First, let me share the positive things that I have experienced in 2020. I took the Ministers Class and found it to be very enlightening but not a challenge. I enjoyed the instruction, interaction, and assignments. I received an A. The year 2020 was an eye-opener motivating me to do more, be more, and accomplish greater spiritual growth spiritually. In lieu of the affected and challenged mindset brought on by the worldwide epidemic/pandemic, I have chosen to be positive and grateful for health and life. *Colossians 2:7 NKJV is rooted and built up in Him and established in the faith, as you have been taught, abounding in it with thanksgiving.* I am extremely thankful for the quality time it allowed me to spend with my family. Moreover, my father, aged 95, and his contact outpouring of wisdom and love of family. I have also decided to extend my experiences in *Crumbs for Life* succeeding COVID.

After slightly over a year of teleworking, virtual funerals, and social distancing, it was hard flipping the script and returning to the workplace. Although it was a challenge, I prepared my mind, heart, and spirit to return with a positive focus. I had an expectation of a changed environment and culture after a year of significant sickness, disease, deaths and painful consequences of family and friends being separated.

As I have assessed in the reunification, many individuals appear not to be humbled by the experience, and it is business as usual. Too many times, I witness detestable verbal responses and actions. People say and do things that are totally unbelievable in a Christian environment. Again, I know that we are all a work in progress. I just believe that the previous year should shed some light on the fact that we are not in control of anything. These very same people proclaim salvation yet perform hateful acts versus praiseworthy and fruitful behavior. Were some people not impacted by what we survived in 2020? For me, many are too relaxed in the Christian environment. Billions did not make it to see 2021, and many are still suffering from COVID or the aftermath and impact of the disease.

I have paid close attention to my surroundings and people in their public displays of chaos and uncontrolled behavior. Seemingly, people are out of captivity and have gone buck wild, reckless driving, unfocused while crossing streets or in parking lots. How do we, as Christians, manage not to be agitated and remain peaceful? I tell you how with constant prayer and communication with God. Faith and love are vital and crucial for survival.

Proverbs 1:5 (NKJV)

A wise man will hear and increase learning, and a man of understanding will attain wise counsel.

Value the time that God has blessed you with. You survived 2020 on purpose. God has a continued plan and if you are not in your calling, know that you are in His radar. He is giving you every opportunity to seek His purpose and goal for your purpose in life. There is work for all of us to do. First your call is to worship Him, serve Him, honor Him by being grateful and giving all glory to Him in all that you do. Surely, this present pandemic is not the last. The Book of Revelation speaks of the seven last plagues and is this the first of them?

Revelation 15-16 NKJV

15 Then I saw another sign in heaven, great and marvelous: seven angels having the seven last plagues, for in them the wrath of God is complete.

If so, we all must prepare ourselves for the many to come as well as the end. Are you ready? Are you aligned in the position God has called you to be? Get ready and stay ready, for we have seen the result of the twist in a world that came like a thief in the night.

Be Specific

E very child looks forward to a celebration and gifts on their birthday. When they are asked what they want, most are specific in the request. If what they asked for was not gifted there was some level of disappointment. Although the parent knew what their child specifically asked for, they also knew what was best for them.

We ask God for forgiveness for many things we say and things we have done. Are we specific in what we ask for forgiveness for? Sometimes, we are not and ask God for forgiveness for anything we have done that is not pleasing in His sight. There may be a specific thing that you bypass, thinking you are hiding it from God, but of course, anyone who believes knows that God sees all, hears all, and is fully aware of all our sins and transgressions.

Many times, those secret things we bypass are the challenges we struggled with and may still be a conflicting stronghold. If you think you have control over things that still jeopardize your walk and relationship with God. That thing, that person still has power.

Facing a weakness and asking for God's power and strength in desires that are contrary to His commands enables you to be specific. Acknowledge it, then ask God to forgive you for your weakness and ask for deliverance from whatever you fall short in. He has all the power and can.

Always be specific in the things we ask in Jesus' name……….. Amen

Philippians 4:6-7 NKJV

Be anxious for nothing, but in everything by prayer and supplication, with thanksgiving, let your requests be made known to God; and the peace of God, which surpasses all understanding, will guard your hearts and minds through Christ Jesus.

Romans 12:12 NKJV

12 rejoicing in hope, patient in tribulation, continuing steadfastly in prayer.

2 Corinthians 10:3-5 NKJV

3 For though we walk in the flesh, we do not war according to the flesh.

4 For the weapons of our warfare are not [a]carnal but mighty in God for pulling down strongholds,

5 casting down arguments and every high thing that exalts itself against the knowledge of God, bringing every thought into captivity to the obedience of Christ.

A Given Sign

M̲ost people know the meaning of street signs. On average, they are duplicated across the nation. However, there may be some signs posted only in areas that require specific attention or maybe a warning. All signs serve purpose and it is up to us to take heed and respond accordingly.

In the year 2020, the world was given a warning sign. We are given signs daily. Signs of the times, but it was not like any other sign we have received thus far. God commanded a pestilence amongst the land. This pandemic caused a massive shut-down, 4,885,778 deaths, according to the world o meter as of October 13th, 2021.

This global outbreak caused the majority to be still and take heed of what we were facing. Many continued to ignore and wanted to function on the previous normal for whatever their personal reasoning. As time passed by and a vaccine was developed, some were receptive, and many were not and still refused to be vaccinated. Some for religious beliefs and some for mere rumors and nonfactual foolishness. Nonetheless, many continued to attend and have events that are categorized as super spreaders.

The number of vaccinated people was on the rise and the economical commodity suffering caused the political population to implement reopening for the economic good!!! The almighty dollar $$$ superseded the signs. God said BE STILL. "If My people which are called by my name humble themselves and pray and seek My face and turn from their wicked ways, then they will hear from heaven, and I will forgive them of their sin. I will heal their land!"

We are not still, and a series of variants are populating one by one; booster vaccines are being given, but humility continues to decline. Do we, the believers, read, comprehend, and understand God's Word and signs? Exodus 9:14 14 For this time I will send all my plagues on you yourself, and on your servants and your people, so that you may know that there is none like me in all the earth.

We must first acknowledge the signs and know that panicking is not the answer, God is in control. Many times, in God's Word, we are reminded not to fear. Trust God, be mindful, use wisdom, take measures to avoid exposure to disease. Pray continually and know that all things work together for the good of God.

2 Chronicles 7:13-14

13 When I shut up the heavens so that there is no rain, or command the locust to devour the land, or send pestilence among my people,

14 if my people who are called by my name humble themselves, and pray and seek my face and turn from their wicked ways, then I will hear from heaven and will forgive their sin and heal their land.

Luke 21:11

11 There will be great earthquakes, and in various places famines and pestilences. And there will be terrors and great signs from heaven.

Romans 11:36

36 For from him and through him and to him are all things. To him be glory forever. Amen.

Church Idols

T he things that stir our passion can easily become the things we idolize. With a sincere heart pursuing and intending to please God by fulfilling His purpose, one can still be distracted. A leader, a ministry, or a group, and sometimes the building can sway you from your first love.

The tenacity, perseverance, and deliberate ambition to develop disciples for God by a leader may cause people to worship him/her. The extraordinary dynamics of the worship place (Church) may cause people to worship the building. Sometimes, a group and the desire to be accepted may cause idolization of the group/ministry as you seek their approval.

We can emulate our leaders but should not idolize them. People, unfortunately, are more concerned with what the Pastor will say or think than God. Honor and respect your Pastor and Leaders, respect the Worship place and the Ministries or groups of your Church. Never worship or idolize people, places, or things. God requires exclusive devotion.

God clearly commands us to place no other God before Him. Examine your passion!!! Therefore, if knowingly or unknowingly, you are worshiping and idolizing the wrong things, repentance is in order. Seek God's forgiveness and truly worship

Him from your heart and all your being. God is worthy of ALL Honor and ALL Praise in His Infinite Glory. He is the Great I Am.

Exodus 20:1-8 (NKJV)

1 And God spoke all these words, saying:

2 "I am the Lord your God, who brought you out of the land of Egypt, out of the house of bondage.

3 "You shall have no other gods before Me.

4 "You shall not make for yourself a carved image—any likeness of anything that is in heaven above, or that is in the earth beneath, or that is in the water under the earth;

5 you shall not bow down to them nor serve them. For I, the Lord your God, am a jealous God, visiting the iniquity of the fathers upon the children to the third and fourth generations of those who hate Me,

6 but showing mercy to thousands, to those who love Me and keep My commandments.

7 "You shall not take the name of the Lord your God in vain, for the Lord will not hold him guiltless who takes His name in vain. 8 "Remember the Sabbath day, to keep it holy.

Deuteronomy 6:4-5 (NKJV)

4 "Hear, O Israel: The Lord our God, the Lord is one!

5 You shall love the Lord your God with all your heart, with all your soul, and with all your strength.

Matthew 4:10-11 (NKJV)

10 Then Jesus said to him, "Away with you, Satan! For it is written, 'You shall worship the Lord your God, and Him only you shall serve.'"

11 Then the devil left Him, and behold, angels came and ministered to Him.

Colossians 3:5 (NKJV)

5 Therefore put to death your members which are on the earth: fornication, uncleanness, passion, evil desire, and covetousness, which is idolatry.